Crash Course in C, Second Edition

D0521178

Paul Perry
Stephen Potts

Crash Course in C, Second Edition

Library of Congress Catalog No.: 94-67370

ISBN: 1-56529-940-x

97 96 95 94   8 7 6 5 4 3 2 1

Interpretation of the printing code: the rightmost double-digit number is the year of the book's printing; the rightmost single-digit number, the number of the book's printing. For example, a printing code of 94-1 shows that the first printing of the book occurred in 1994.

Publisher: David P. Ewing

Associate Publisher: Michael Miller

Managing Editor: Michael Cunningham

Product Marketing Manager: Greg Weigand

Credits

Publishing Director
Joseph B. Wikert

Acquisitions Editor
Angela J. Lee

Product Development Specialist
Bryan Gambrel

Production Editor
Lori Cates

Editors
Lynn Northrup
Kathy Simpson

Technical Editor
Michael Stanley

Acquisitions Coordinator
Patricia J. Brooks

Editorial Assistant
Michelle Williams

Book Designer
Paula Carroll

Cover Designer
Jean Bisesi

Graphic Image Specialists
Teresa Forrester
Tim Montgomery
Dennis Sheehan
Susan VandeWalle

Production Team
Steve Adams
Claudia Bell
Cameron Booker
Stephen Carlin
DiMonique Ford
Joelynn Gifford
Dennis Clay Hager
Bob LaRoche
Steph Mineart
Mary Beth Wakefield
Angelina Ward

Indexer
Michael Hughes

Composed in *Stone Serif* and *MCPdigital*
by Macmillan Computer Publishing

Dedications

To my sister, Amy, for being such a fun person to be around.
—P.P.

To my son, James, who loves computers.
—S.P.

We'd Like To Hear from You!

As part of our continuing effort to produce books of the highest possible quality, Que would like to hear your comments. To stay competitive, we *really* want you, as a computer book reader and user, to let us know what you like or dislike most about this book or other Que products.

You can mail comments, ideas, or suggestions for improving future editions to the address below, or send us a fax at (317) 581-4663. For the on-line inclined, Macmillan Computer Publishing now has a forum on CompuServe (type **GO QUEBOOKS** at any prompt) through which our staff and authors are available for questions and comments. In addition to exploring our forum, please feel free to contact me personally on CompuServe at 75230,1556 to discuss your opinions of this book.

Thanks in advance—your comments will help us to continue publishing the best books available on computer topics in today's market.

Bryan Gambrel
Product Development Specialist
Que Corporation
201 W. 103rd Street
Indianapolis, Indiana 46290
U.S.A.

About the Authors

Paul J. Perry has been programming for more than five years. He is the author of a number of books related to programming in C and C++ for both DOS and Windows. Mr. Perry was a technical support engineer for Borland International, where he helped customers find answers to their consulting questions for a support program called the Borland Advisor Line. At Borland he was also in charge of support forums on CompuServe, and was involved in writing technical support information sheets for customers. His current job is as a Windows multimedia programming specialist at a well-known consumer electronics company.

Stephen Potts received a degree in Computer Science from Georgia Tech. He has been designing and writing software systems for 12 years. He is a consultant in Windows-based technologies and owns NoBoredom Classes, a computer education firm in Atlanta.

Acknowledgments

From Paul J. Perry:

Thanks to the fabulous team at Que, including Joe Wikert and all the other people behind the scenes. It could not have been done without you.

From Stephen Potts:

I'd like to thank Angela Lee and Joe Wikert of Que for their continued support.

Trademarks

All terms mentioned in this book that are known to be trademarks or service marks have been appropriately capitalized. Que cannot attest to the accuracy of this information. Use of a term in this book should not be regarded as affecting the validity of any trademark or service mark.

Screen reproductions in this book were created using Collage Complete from Inner Media, Inc., Hollis, NH.

Contents at a Glance

Contents

4 Keyboard Input and Video Output　　　　49

5 Programs that Make Decisions　　　　69

12 Bitwise Operators   217

Index   235

Introduction

Most major software developers use the C programming language to write their applications. C has become the most popular programming language in existence.

Virtually all the current books about C programming are large, comprehensive books that explore every aspect of the language. This book teaches only the essential elements of C programming. *Crash Course in C*, Second Edition, offers the reader a *fast* way to learn the C programming language.

This book takes a "no-frills" approach to teaching the most important aspects of the C language. You start learning C in the first chapter. This book focuses on the key features of the language. It enables the reader to begin writing practical applications in the shortest amount of time possible.

Who Should Use This Book?

This book is aimed at readers who want to learn the C programming language in the shortest amount of time possible. The audience includes non-programmers who can learn in a fast-track environment as well as programmers who are switching to C.

What You Should Know to Use This Book

This book assumes that you are familiar with common computer terminology. Time is not wasted teaching you what an ASCII code is or how to write a batch file to start a C compiler. You should have a good grasp of basic computing principles before reading this book.

Although programming experience is not necessary, it is helpful if you have programmed (even a little) in some computer language. Whether you have worked with FORTRAN, BASIC, or Pascal, the knowledge you already have helps you get up to speed in C.

Organization of This Book

Crash Course in C, Second Edition, is divided into 12 chapters. Each chapter covers a fundamental aspect of the language. You start with programming basics and move to every essential element of C programming. Table I.1 summarizes the contents of each chapter.

Chapter	Contents
1	History and basic structure of the C language
2	Example program, explained step by step
3	Description and purpose of C variables and operators
4	How to get keyboard input and display video output
5	An examination of decision-making statements
6	Discussion of C's looping statements
7	Explanation of functions and how they are used
8	Description of C preprocessor directives
9	Information about pointers and other data types
10	How to use advanced data structures
11	How to access disk files in C
12	How to use bitwise operators

Table I.1 The Organization of *Crash Course in C*

By the end of this book, you will be familiar with the important concepts of C programming and will be able to speak intelligently about the subject.

Notation and Conventions

To get the most out of this book, you should know how it is designed. New terms and emphasized words are presented in *italicized text* and are defined on first reference. Pay close attention to italicized text. Functions, commands, parameters, and the like are set in `monospace` text; for example, the `main()` function. User responses that must be typed at the prompt appear in **`monospace bold`**, for example:

```
Please Enter Your Name: Kevin
```

Placeholders (words that you replace with actual values) in code lines appear in *`monospace italic`;* for example:

```
long double variable1, variable2;
```

In this example, you would replace *`variable1`* and *`variable2`* with appropriate names, depending, of course, on the program you were writing.

Full C programs appear as listings with listing heads, whereas code fragments appear alone within the text. These listings have been tested using the Borland C++ 4.0 compiler. However, all of the code is ANSI C, so no matter what operating system or compiler you are using, the examples should compile.

Throughout the book, you will also see *Syntax* shaded boxes with the syntax icon. This design feature provides easy language reference to the essential elements of C programming. By providing this helpful information, the book will serve not only as a tutorial, but as a reference that you can turn back to.

The Syntax Box

This is a Syntax box. It provides syntax explanations for C functions and procedures. You can use this information repeatedly as a quick reference to the C language syntax.

The box first shows you the standard format of the function or procedure, like so:

```
standard function (goes here);
```

A few examples generally follow, like the following:

```
standard function (get)
standard function (put)
standard function (if)
```

For more information about the function, read the text surrounding the box.

Other visual pointers found in this book include the following:

Caution

Caution boxes warn you of problem areas, including possible cases in which you might introduce bugs into your program or crash your system.

Note

Note boxes provide you with extraneous information. Many times, this information will help speed your learning process and show you shortcuts in C. Other times, it simply reminds you of information important enough to be mentioned twice!

Tip
This is an example of a Tip.

In addition to Notes and Cautions, this book also includes Tips in the margins. These Tips show you shorter, easier ways of doing things. An example of a Tip is next to this paragraph.

Learn by Doing

There is an important rule about programming: *You learn by doing!* Trying an example is one of the best ways to learn. It is impossible to learn C without writing code, compiling your programs, and observing the way they work.

Writing programs is essential to learning the C language; the example programs are included for you to try. However, you should try your own examples as well. It is imperative to experiment with a language to really learn it, and C is no exception.

So, with all this out of the way, you can begin your discovery of C programming.

Chapter 1

C Programming Basics

C is a general-purpose, structured programming language that can be used for a broad variety of programming tasks. The C language is characterized by its capability to produce concise source code programs. This is, in part, due to the large number of *operators* (symbols that cause a program to do something to its variables) included in the language. Furthermore, most implementations of the language have a rather extensive library of *functions* (sections of code that perform specific tasks) that enhance the basic language definition.

C resembles other high-level structured programming languages such as Pascal and Modula-2; however, C contains features that enable programmers to use it at a lower level as well. In this way, it bridges the gap between machine language and high-level structured languages.

History of C

C was originally designed and implemented in 1972 by Dennis Ritchie at Bell Telephone Laboratories, Inc. (now AT&T Bell Laboratories), and outlined in the book *The C Programming Language,* by Brian Kernighan and Dennis Ritchie. C was an outgrowth of two earlier languages—BCPL and B—also developed at Bell Laboratories.

Because of its general usefulness in developing operating systems, device drivers, and other types of system software, the language has sometimes been called a "system programming language." C combines high-level language constructions with the capability to interact with the operating system at a low level.

As developers began programming in C, different dialects of the language started appearing on different computing platforms. This happened because parts of the language weren't clearly defined, so they were interpreted differently by each compiler implementation. It was clear that C needed to be updated so that an industry standard could be established.

In 1983, the *American National Standards Institute* (ANSI) established a committee to create a standard definition of the C programming language. The committee included professors, researchers, and programmers from some of the top computer companies. In 1988, the second edition of the book by Kernighan and Ritchie (by this time known as K&R) was published. It included the standardized version of C, called *ANSI C*.

Types of C Compilers

All modern C *compilers* (programs that convert the C language into instructions that are executed by the microprocessor) support the ANSI standard version of C. Many compilers also provide additional language enhancements. These enhancements are either dependent on the computer on which they are being used or are additions to the language that make C easier to use.

If you purchase a compiler from Borland International or Microsoft Corporation, you receive special *compiler extensions* that make C easier to use on PC-based systems. These compilers almost always have an option that disables any compiler extensions, making C compile the code only in accordance with ANSI specifications. For the examples in this book, you will want to do this.

When you program in accordance with the ANSI standard, your code is *portable* to other operating systems. This means the code can run with little or no modification on different systems. This is a valuable characteristic because as you program, you may need to be able to use your application on different computer systems. Doing so opens up large markets for your software. The less hassle and time it takes when converting your code to different systems, the more time you can spend adding functionality to your program—or vacationing in Tahiti.

Today, many vendors sell C++ compilers instead of C compilers. The C++ language is a *superset* of C. This means that programs written in C++ have all the features of C, plus more. Therefore, if you buy a C++ compiler, you can still compile C programs. Furthermore, you have the ability to move on to C++ and object-oriented programming in the future, as your needs expand.

> **Note**
>
> Don't be scared about buying a C++ compiler. The C++ compiler suits all your needs and provides more features for the future.

Why Code in C?

There must be some reasons for the popularity of C. Although C can be difficult to use, it also has many strong points. As you begin using C, you will recognize many of the following virtues:

- C is often called a *middle-level language.* The C programming language is a middle-level language because it combines elements of high-level languages (such as Pascal and FORTRAN) with functions of assembly language (the capability to work at the lowest level of the computer). This is important because it enables you to work with an easy-to-understand language, and still accomplish tasks that could previously only be done with cryptic instructions to the microprocessor.

- The C programming language is a *structured language.* The idea of a structured language is that you can break your code into small chunks and put each chunk of code into its own subprogram (or function). Your main program is then made up of multiple subprograms. Each subprogram has its own logic and is like its own program. This is valuable because a structured programming language enables you to create large-scale programs.

- C is code efficient. Programs in C can be written in several lines, whereas other languages might consume half a page to accomplish the same task (assuming the task can be done in the other language).

- Programs written in C are *portable.* As stated earlier, this means that C programs written on one system can run with little or no modification on other systems. Compilers for C are available on just about every operating system.

- The C programming language is powerful and flexible. C is not meant to be easy to read or simple to understand. Its sole purpose is to enable the programmer to have access to all levels of the computer.

If you ever become discouraged while learning C, remember that word processors, spreadsheets, arcade-style games, and operating systems all have been written in C. If these other programmers were able to learn C, you can too.

Compiled and Interpreted Languages

If your programming experience has been limited to BASIC, you might find some of the operations in C rather strange. Program development tools are divided into two broad categories: *interpreted* and *compiled* languages. BASIC is an interpreted language, whereas C is a compiled language.

A program written in a high-level language must be translated into machine language before it can be executed. *Compilers* (such as C and Pascal) translate an entire program into machine language before executing any of the instructions. *Interpreters* (which is how the BASIC language is usually implemented) proceed through a program by first translating each line and then executing the instructions, one instruction at a time—slowly making its way through the program.

A compiler is a computer program that accepts a high-level program (such as a C program) as input and generates a corresponding machine-language program as output. The original high-level program is called the *source code,* and the resulting machine-language program is called the *object code.* Another program combines the object code and creates an executable file. This process is known as *linking.* See figure 1.1 for a visual representation of these processes.

Fig. 1.1
The processes of editing, compiling, linking, and running your programs.

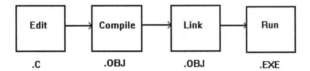

Every high-level language must have a compiler or interpreter. If you have used GW-BASIC, BASICA, or QBASIC, you have used an interpreter. Most implementations of C operate as compilers. Pascal and FORTRAN are also compiled languages. Several languages have both interpreters and compilers available for them.

Interpreted languages are usually more convenient to use during program development. However, once a program is error-free, a compiled version of the program normally executes much faster than an interpreted version. Most importantly, the compiled version of the program only has to be accompanied with the resulting machine-language program since your source code was not distributed.

An interpreted language requires that you distribute the source code of the program. You may consider that code a company asset, and not want customers to see it. Interpreted languages often require that the language interpreter be present at run time. This may impose an unreasonable cost on the customer.

Writing the Code

When you write a program in C, you first use an editor to store the text of the program into an ASCII text file. This text file is referred to as the program's *source file*. The first part of the file name, the *prefix*, is the name of the program (for example, MYPROG). On PC-based systems, you are limited to eight characters for each file name prefix. Other operating systems allow more characters.

In most cases, you also give C source files an extension (or *suffix*) of ".c". This reminds the compiler (and you) that the file comprises C source code. The results are file names such as HELLO.C, FIRST.C, and MYPROG.C.

Compiling the Program

Once you have a program, you want to run it. In order to do this, you must first compile the file. The compiler converts your source code to an intermediate file, called the *object module*.

After you compile the program, the object module file is created. The *object module* is an intermediate file with an OBJ extension. The object module is simply a form of assembly language. However, there are several things missing from the object module. First, any library functions that your program calls are not included in this file. Second, the code that begins the program, called the *start-up code*, is not included in the object module. Before you can run it, these missing pieces must be added.

Although the object module contains assembly language, it is not ready to be executed. To execute the file, it must be combined with the start-up code and the library functions that your program uses. Doing so will create a program file.

Linking Your Code

The linking process combines your OBJ file with the start-up code and library functions into a final program. The final program has an extension of EXE on PC-based computers. Other operating systems may use different file extensions.

Running the File

You can run the executable file by typing its file name at the command-line prompt. At that point, you see the fruits of your labor.

Compilers from Borland International contain an *Integrated Development Environment* (IDE) that includes a built-in editor, a compiler, and a linker. This way, you can use the editor to write your source code. You can then make a selection from a menu; your program is compiled into an object module, linked into a final EXE, and executed, all in one simple step.

As you might guess, the Integrated Development Environment (IDE) has helped the productivity of programmers by making program development much easier. It reduces the time necessary to manually compile, link, and execute a program.

Debugging and Testing Your Program

If you have programmed before, you know that many programs don't run the first time you execute them. The process of getting your program to run is known as *debugging*.

> **Caution**
>
> Even if you have a running program, you must test it to make sure it works as you expected. On simple programs, this can be as easy as executing it once and making sure the results are acceptable. On a system that will be sold commercially, you may spend hundreds of hours testing and fixing your code.

Testing larger programs might require the help of your key customers. When a program goes into this testing stage, it is usually referred to as *beta testing*. Beta testing can be a valuable step in program development because you receive feedback from people who are using your program on a daily basis and are doing real-life activities. They will discover bugs that you never would.

Summary

This chapter gave you a basic understanding of the C programming language. It discussed the history and benefits of C, informed you about some of the types of C compilers available, introduced the concept of compiled and interpreted languages, and briefly explained the processes of editing, compiling, linking, running, and debugging programs.

The following points were covered in this chapter:

- The *C programming language* was developed by Brian Kernighan and Dennis Ritchie from AT&T Bell Labs.

- *ANSI C* is the standard definition of the language prepared by the American National Standards Institute. It provides a standard on which all C compilers can be based.

- Every program written in a high-level language must be translated into machine language before it can be executed. The two broad categories of software translation tools are *interpreters* and *compilers*.

- In an *interpreted language,* the interpreter proceeds through a program by translating and then executing single instructions, one at a time.

- In a *compiled language,* the high-level program instructions are translated all at once. The resulting machine-language program is linked and then executed when you want to run the program.

- In order to execute a program on your computer, you must first compile it. This creates an intermediate file called an *object module.* The object module is then linked with the compiler's libraries to create an executable program.

Chapter 2

Your First Program

This chapter presents your first C program. You learn what each statement in the program does and how it relates to C programming in general. Each of the concepts covered in this chapter is described in more detail in later chapters. By the end of this chapter, you should begin to understand how C programming works.

Starting with an Example

Listing 2.1 presents your first C program. Take a quick look at the program. Create a source file by entering the listing into a text editor. Then compile, link, and run the program.

Listing 2.1   Your First C Program

```
/**************************************
 FIRST.C - Your first C program
           Program to calculate the
           area of a circle.
**************************************/

#include <stdio.h>

#define PI 3.1415

int main()
{
   float area, radius;

   printf("Please Enter Radius: ");
   scanf("%f", &radius);

   area = PI * radius * radius;

   printf("The Area is %f\n", area);

   return 0;
}
```

Listing 2.1 is an elementary C program that accepts the radius of a circle from the user, calculates the circle's area, then displays the calculated results.

When you run the program, it produces output similar to the following:

```
Please Enter Radius: 3
The Area is 28.273500
```

The user entered the **3** as the radius and the program provided the result. Take a look at each part of the program.

Learning the Elements of a C Program

The same basic components are necessary to create every C program. All C programs follow the same basic structure. Even a large, complex C program generally has the same layout as a short one. The following elements are found in most C programs:

- Preprocessor directives
- Variables
- Declarations
- Function declarations
- The `main()` function

Before you find out about the exact statements in the program, you should know a little bit about the general syntax of C.

Case Sensitivity

It is important to know that C is a case-sensitive language. This means that upper- and lowercase letters are treated as separate characters. For example, the names TOTAL, total, Total, and totaL are all treated as different identifiers. Languages such as BASIC and Pascal, on the other hand, are not case-sensitive and treat these names in exactly the same way.

> **Caution**
>
> When you type a C program into the compiler, be careful to use the proper case. If you don't, the compiler will not recognize your code and the program will not be processed correctly.

The C Character Set

C uses the uppercase letters A to Z, the lowercase letters a to z, the digits 0 to 9, and the following special characters:

[	]	{	}	<	>	(	)
!	*	+	=	"	'	.	?
#	/	\	&	%	-	_	^
~	¦	;	:	,	@	$	`

C uses a combination of these characters to represent special operations. Some might be obvious (such as the addition (+) operator); others are not. They are defined in the book as they are introduced.

Using Comments in Your Program

Comments are an important part of any program. They help the person writing a program, and anyone else who must read the source file, to understand what's happening. All comments are ignored by the compiler, so they do not add to the size of the final executable program. Neither do they affect the execution time of the executable program.

A comment is not a required part of a program. It does not perform any programming task. Comments can be used freely throughout your program to make the code easier to understand.

> **Note**
>
> Adding comments to your code is a valuable habit to adopt. When you look at old code, comments help refresh your memory as to the purpose of each section of code. Use comments throughout your code as much as possible. If there is ever a question in your mind as to whether to add a comment, always add it.

In C, comments begin with the sequence /* and are terminated by the sequence */. Everything within the markers is ignored. In the FIRST.C program, the first several lines of the program are comments, as follows:

```
/****************************************
 FIRST.C - Your first C program
           Program to calculate the
           area of a circle.
 ****************************************/
```

Helpful information to provide in the comments at the beginning of your program includes the author's name, the date the program was written, and any revision notes.

Including Preprocessor Directives

You can include various instructions to the C compiler in the source code of your program. These instructions are called *preprocessor directives*. Although they are not strictly part of the C language, they expand the scope of C in useful ways. All preprocessor directives begin with the pound (#) character.

The preprocessor directives are interpreted before the compilation process begins. Preprocessor directives usually appear at the beginning of a program and are grouped with other directives, although this is not required. The directives precede the code to which they refer.

The following line from FIRST.C instructs the compiler to include information about the standard input/output library:

```
#include <stdio.h>
```

This line appears at the beginning of many C source code files.

The `#include` directive instructs the compiler to include another source file in the file that contains the directive. The source file you want to include is enclosed in angle brackets. Figure 2.1 shows the effect of the `#include` directive.

In C, the file included in your code (in this case, stdio.h) is called the *header file,* or simply the *header.* The file has this name because declarations are usually found at the beginning of a program.

Fig. 2.1
The effect of adding the *#include* directive to your file.

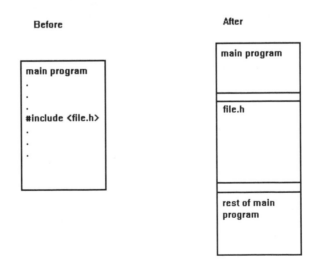

The other preprocessor directive in the FIRST.C program, as follows, is called a definition statement:

```
#define PI 3.1415
```

When the preprocessor scans the source code, it replaces all instances of PI with the number 3.1415. This is a similar concept to a constant declaration.

Understanding the *main()* Function

Notice the main() function in listing 2.1. The section of code starting with main() and enclosed in braces is called a *function*. Every C program consists of one or more functions, one of which must be called main(). Program execution always begins with the main() function.

> **Note**
>
> The parentheses after the main() function inform the compiler that the program is calling a function. Even if a function does not pass any values to a function, main() still must have the empty parentheses.

All C programs are divided into small, separate units known as *functions*. Most high-level computer languages break programs into small units like this. Sometimes these smaller units are called *subprograms*.

FORTRAN and BASIC use subroutines. Pascal, being more similar to C, uses procedures and functions. There are obvious differences between how other languages operate, but the main idea of using the concept of functions is the same.

A C program is a collection of functions—each program is composed of one or more functions. Each function, then, contains one or more C statements. A function usually carries out a single task. Each function has a name and a list of values that the function receives. Most of the time, you can give a function any name you want. As you will see shortly, the main() function is a special case.

A C program can have almost an unlimited number of functions. No matter how many functions exist, the main() function always receives control from the operating system when the program begins to run. All C programs must have a main() function because it is executed first every time your program begins to run.

Your program can have only one main() function. If you have more than one main(), the compiler does not know which to use. If you don't believe me, include more than one `main()` statement in your program and try to compile it. It won't work!

A *function definition* informs the compiler of the name of the function. When you learn more about functions, you will see that functions interact with values used in the program. In the FIRST.C program, the function definition is

```
int main()
```

The keyword `int` tells the compiler that the function returns an integer value. The word `main()` is the name of the function, and the parentheses tell the compiler that the programmer is creating the body of the function.

Some programs have only one function (like the one in listing 2.1). Large programs become too complex if you try to put all of the code inside a single function. Large programs should break tasks into logical steps, each of which is carried out in a function. Calls to the separate functions, then, are found inside `main()`.

Following the function definition are curly braces that signal the beginning and end of the function. The opening brace ({) signifies that a block of code is about to begin. The closing brace (}) terminates a block of code. In C, braces perform a similar function to the `Begin...End` statements in Pascal. In essence, braces mark the body of a function.

Learning the Parts of the Program

This section looks at the statements found inside the braces of the `main()` function. These statements are the code lines that actually compose the program.

Declaring Variables

Inside the `main()` function declaration, you see a line that reads:

```
float area, radius;
```

This statement declares two floating-point variables. The names of the variables are `area` and `radius`. The keyword `float` signifies that the variables are to contain a decimal point. A variable is a symbolic name that can be assigned different values.

Displaying Output

To display text on the current output device (usually a video monitor), use a statement like this:

```
printf("Please Enter Radius: ");
```

This line is actually a call to another function. It is the formatted print or printf() function. The printf() function takes the argument passed to it—in this case a string constant—and outputs the argument to the standard output device. Because you included the stdio.h file, which declares standard input and output functions, the string is displayed on the video monitor.

Getting Input

To get input from the user, use the scanf() function, as follows:

```
scanf("%f", &radius);
```

The scanf() function can be used to enter any combination of numerical values and single characters. This function returns the number of data items entered successfully.

When you call the scanf() function, you pass two parameters to it. The first is known as a *control string* and always appears inside quotation marks. The control string tells the compiler what types of numbers you want the user to enter. In this program, the %f refers to a floating-point number. The second parameter in the scanf() function specifies which variable should receive the value entered by the user.

The Body of the Program

The main calculation of the program looks like this:

```
area = PI * radius * radius;
```

Remember that PI is actually a preprocessor directive that is replaced by a number. Thus, the line the compiler reads appears like this:

```
area = 3.1415 * radius * radius;
```

This line is an assignment statement that multiplies the number 3.1415 with the value stored in the variable radius, then multiplies the product by the value stored in radius again. The result is stored in the variable named area.

Finally, to output the results to the user, the printf() function is used like this:

```
printf("The Area is %f\n", area);
```

This line calls the printf() function again. However, this call is a little different. Notice that two parameters are passed to the function and that the funny %f character appears again.

The %f is used here as it was in the scanf() function, with one exception. Instead of inputting a floating-point number from the user, you use this character to display a number as a floating-point value on-screen. The number you want to display is stored in the variable named area and, coincidentally, area shows up as the last parameter to the function.

The \n after the %f characters is an *escape character*. It sends a carriage return and line-feed combination to the screen. The escape character causes your program to move the cursor to the next line on-screen.

Returning

The last statement before the closing curly brace inside the program is

```
return 0;
```

The return statement exits the current function. In this case, the statement returns the program to the operating system, then passes a return value to the operating system. When exiting from the main() function, the return value shows an error value. Listing 2.1 returns 0, denoting that no error occurred.

Listing 2.1 initially defined main() so it would return only an integer value (remember the declaration, int main(), at the beginning of the program?). The error code value can be checked by a batch file that can, in turn, cause different programs to be executed.

The ANSI definition of the language requires that the main() function return an integer value. In practice, the return value is not used much. In fact, if you turn off ANSI compatibility, most compilers enable you to declare main() to return no value.

Learning More About C

All C and C++ compilers come with an extensive set of built-in library functions that help you write your programs. The printf() and scanf() functions are just two of these library functions. Because the compiler provides a number of ready-to-run library functions, you can use the compiler more quickly than if you had to write your own functions.

Notice that every line of the program inside the braces is terminated with a semicolon (;). In C, statements are separated with the semicolon. It is this semicolon that separates one line from the next on the screen.

The C programming language does not recognize "whitespace" characters—carriage returns, tabs, and spaces. You can put as many whitespace characters in your program as you like. It does not matter to the C compiler (except within a literal string). In fact, the whitespace characters are invisible to the compiler.

> **Note**
>
> Whitespace characters are recognized by C only within a literal string. Because whitespace is not recognized anywhere else, use it liberally in your program to improve readability.

Listing 2.1, FIRST.C, would compile and run exactly the same if you had entered it in the following format:

```
int main()
{
  float area, radius;printf("Please Enter Radius: ");
  scanf("%f", &radius);area = PI * radius * radius;
  printf("The Area is %f\n", area);return 0;
}
```

Similarly, the program would run the same if it had the following format:

```
int main(){float area,
     radius;printf("Please Enter Radius: ");
scanf("%f", &radius);area = PI * radius * radius;
printf("The Area is %f\n", area);return 0;}
```

Although the two preceding examples are treated the same by the compiler, the code obviously looks different to programmers. The second example makes the program structure difficult to spot. The first appearance of the program (in listing 2.1) is the easiest of the three methods for humans to understand.

Because the compiler is so flexible, C programmers are able to use their own programming styles. All programs conform to a similar style throughout this book. The most important style point to adopt is the alignment of matching braces. This procedure makes it easier to ensure that every opening brace has a closing brace. Also, the program is usually spaced so that it's easier to understand.

Summary

This chapter examined the basic structure of a typical C program. You learned about preprocessor directives, program variables, C statements, and the main entry point of a C program.

In particular, you learned the following topics:

- Elements of a C program include *preprocessor directives, variable declarations, function declarations,* and the `main()` *function.* The `main()` function receives control when the program begins to run. There can be only *one* `main()` function in every program.

- The C programming language is *case-sensitive;* that is, it treats upper- and lowercase letters separately. The identifiers LANGUAGE, Language, languagE, and LaNgUaGe are each unique and different to a C program.

- *Comments* are used in a C program to help humans understand exactly what is happening in the code. Comments are ignored by the compiler. They begin with the /* characters and end with the */ characters.

■ *Preprocessor directives* begin with a pound sign (#) and give instructions to the C preprocessor. They are carried out before the compiler compiles the code. The #include preprocessor directive is used to include a file in another file. The included file is usually called a header file.

■ *Curly braces* signal a block of code. The opening brace ({) signifies the beginning of a block of code. The closing brace (}) terminates a block of code.

■ Every statement in a C program is terminated with a semicolon (;) character. Whitespace characters (carriage returns, tabs, and spaces) are not recognized by the C programming language as terminators.

Chapter 3

Variables and Operators

A C program consists of variables, functions, and operators. These are the fundamental parts of any computer language. A *variable* is a symbolic name to which different values can be assigned. A *function* is a section of code that performs a particular operation (discussed in Chapter 7, "Modular Programming with Functions"). *Operators* are words or symbols that cause a program to take action on a variable.

A variable is stored in the computer's memory. When a variable receives a value, that value is placed in the memory space designated for the symbol that corresponds to the variable. Different types of variables require different amounts of memory storage. Like most computer languages, C supports several different types of variables. Unlike other computer languages, however, C allows great versatility in declaring variable types. The first part of this chapter explains C variables and data types.

The C programming language includes a large number of operators that fall into several different categories. The second half of this chapter examines the most common operators. Specifically, you will see how assignment operators, arithmetic operators, relational tests, and logical operators are used to form expressions.

Using Variables

All variables in C must be declared before they are used. (Pascal is another language that has this requirement.) Declaring variables is necessary because the compiler must know what type of data a variable holds before it can properly compile other statements that rely on the variable. This process is part of what makes a C compiler efficient compared with languages such as BASIC.

A *data type* is a set of values that represent a particular variable in memory. The C programming language has four basic data types, as follows:

- integer (`int`)
- floating point (`float`)
- double precision (`double`)
- character (`char`)

When declaring your variables, you must consider what the variables will hold and declare them based on this information. The data type of a variable determines what type of data the variable can contain, as well as the range of values that the variable can store.

Variable Declarations

Following is the general format of a variable-declaration statement:

```
VariableType VariableNameList;
```

Here, `VariableType` is a valid C data type, and `VariableNameList` is one or more identifier names separated by commas.

Following are examples of variable declarations:

```
float total;
int x, y;
double a, b, radius;
char ch;
```

The first declaration defines a variable—`total`—to be of type `float` (floating point). The second declaration creates two integer variables named x and y. In C, it is legal to declare multiple variables on one line. Such a declaration saves space and typing time. The third declaration creates three variables of type `double`. The last declaration creates a variable named ch of type `char` (character).

A variable name can consist of letters and digits; the first character must be a letter. Both uppercase and lowercase identifiers are permitted. You also can use the underscore character (_) in a variable declaration. An underscore often is used in the middle of an identifier to make the identifier easier to read (for example, `database_identifier` and `create_icon_indirect`).

In the following sections, you learn the types of variables that C provides. You also learn the difference between constants and variables.

Using Integer Variables

Integers consist of any valid combination of digits along with a plus or minus sign. An *integer* is a number that does not contain a decimal point. Integers in mathematics are whole numbers and can be negative or positive. Examples of integers include the following:

```
1676, -49, 0, 61841, -123
```

Notice that integers can be positive or negative. If a plus sign (+) is not declared, the variable is assumed to be positive. To declare a number negative, you must include the (-) symbol. The number 0 (zero) also is included in the set of integers.

Example integer variable declarations include:

```
int counter;
int x, y, center, radius;
int bikes = 12;
```

To declare an integer, first list the reserved word `int` and then list the names of the variables to be declared. The keyword `int` signals your program to set aside enough space for the integer and to assign the name following the keyword to represent that memory space.

The third declaration in the preceding code sets up a variable named `bikes` and assigns it an initial value. Assigning an initial value to a variable often is very useful. You cannot assume that a variable is assigned any specific value when you first declare it; if you want the variable to have a certain value, you must assign it yourself.

> **Caution**
>
> Using an uninitialized variable can have unpredictable results. Never rely on a variable's having a specific value unless you assign that value to the variable.

Listing 3.1 declares an integer variable and gives it a value. When you execute the program, C creates the variable and assigns it an integer value; that value is displayed on-screen.

Listing 3.1   Using an Integer Variable

```
/************************************************
   INT.C - Uses an integer.
   ************************************************/

#include <stdio.h>

int main()
```

(continues)

Listing 3.1 Continued

```
{
   int x;

   x = 456;
   printf("The value of x is %d\n", x);

   return 0;
}
```

Notice the use of the assignment statement, which assigns the value of 456 to variable x. The equal sign (=) is the assignment operator—it gives the variable on the left side the value of the constant on the right side.

C uses three types of integers: int, short, and long. The int type is the most commonly used integer type. The short type is the same as int on most PC-based C compilers (two bytes). A long integer type is four bytes; therefore, a long variable can hold a much larger value. The three types of integers provide a means of specifying a more exact size or range of values that the variables can hold.

Every int variable requires two bytes of memory and holds numbers in the range –32,768 to 32,767. You will see how this compares with the memory requirements of other variable types as you read about them in this chapter. You will find that two bytes is a rather small amount of memory. For this reason, integers are commonly used as counters in program loops and temporary variables.

Using Floating-Point Variables

Floating-point variables are used when your program uses fractional components or when your application requires extremely large or small numbers. *Floating-point variables* represent numbers with a decimal place. Examples include 3.1415927, .00001676, and 49.678.

C uses three basic types of floating-point numbers: float, double, and long double. The difference between them is the magnitude of the largest, as well as the smallest, number they can hold. The following sections describe these variable types, beginning with float, which is the smallest of the floating-point variable types.

Type *float*

Variables defined as float can be in the range $3.4 \times 10^{+38}$ to 3.4×10^{-38} and can occupy four bytes of memory. Precision is set to seven digits of accuracy.

Floating-point variables require more memory to be stored. As a result, the computer takes longer to process information with a variable declared as `float` or `double`.

Choosing the correct data type is an important aspect of creating optimized programs that run quickly and efficiently. The following examples show several floating-point variable declarations:

```
float diameter;
float principal, interest;
float distance = 25.05;
```

The first declaration is the simplest; it declares a single variable with no initial value. The second declaration shows how to declare multiple variables on a single line. The third declaration shows the assignment of an initial value to the variable.

Listing 3.2 shows how to use floating-point variables in a program. The program prompts the user to enter three weights, and then calculates the average weight.

Listing 3.2   FLOAT.C, a Program that Calculates the Average of Three Weights

```
/******************************************************
  FLOAT.C - Example of using floating-point numbers.
 ******************************************************/

#include <stdio.h>

int main()
{
   float avg;
   float weight1, weight2, weight3;

   printf("Enter first person's weight\n");
   scanf("%f", &weight1);

   printf("Enter second person's weight\n");
   scanf("%f", &weight2);

   printf("Enter third person's weight\n");
   scanf("%f", &weight3);

   avg = (weight1 + weight2 + weight3) / 3;

   printf("Average weight is %f\n", avg);

   return 0;
}
```

A sample interaction with listing 3.2 looks like the following:

```
Enter first person's weight
145
Enter second person's weight
167
Enter third person's weight
130
Average weight is 147.333328
```

You can see how the program inputs the three values and then calculates the average value, depending on which numbers the user enters. Anybody with programming experience would laugh at the efficiency of this program, because the groups of printf() and scanf() functions can be easily executed several times in a loop, which would save repetitive code. Loops, however, aren't covered in this book until Chapter 6, "Programs that Loop." For now, just know that you can use that method.

Type *double*

The second type of floating-point value is double. Variables of type double require eight bytes of memory to be stored and can hold numbers in the range 1.7×10^{-308} to $1.7 \times 10^{+308}$. The larger size provides better precision and range, but also uses more memory. Because they can hold larger values, numbers of type double are often used in scientific and financial calculations.

Examples of double variable declarations follow:

```
double value;
double pi = 3.1415927;
```

The first line creates a double variable with the name value. The second creates a double variable with the name pi and assigns it an initial value.

Type *long double*

A long double requires 10 bytes of memory and can store values in the range 3.4×10^{-4932} to $3.4 \times 10^{+4932}$. A long double requires 10 bytes of memory. The size of the numbers that this variable type can hold depends on the type of compiler you are using. Following are some examples of declarations:

```
long double very_big_number;
long double variable1, variable2;
```

Notice that this variable type requires two keywords. The long keyword actually is a type modifier that modifies the basic definition of the double type. Besides providing a greater array of values to be stored, a long double provides more precise values. A long double has 19 digits of precision.

Using Character Variables

Most variable types are numeric, but the character (char) type isn't. A *character* is a single letter surrounded by single quotation marks (actually, apostrophes). Character variables are used to hold eight-bit ASCII characters, such as 'A', 'P', '1', or any other eight-bit quantity. A character variable uses one byte in memory.

Character variables are used to represent the ASCII character set. An *ASCII code* is a number used to represent a symbol. Sometimes, you will find that variables of type char and type int are similar and can be used interchangeably.

To declare two character variables, use the following statement:

```
char letter1, letter2;
```

You might want to assign special control codes to characters. C defines certain codes that are used to assign a control code to a variable. Table 3.1 displays these special-character constants.

Note

The special-character constants are useful when you have special formatting needs for the output of your program.

Table 3.1 Special-Character Constants

Code	Description
'\a'	Bell
'\\'	Backslash
'\b'	Backspace
'\r'	Carriage return
'\"'	Double quotations
'\f'	Form feed
'\n'	Newline character
'\0'	Null value
'\''	Single quotation
'\t'	Tab
'\v'	Vertical tab

To assign a backslash character to a code, use the following line of code:

```
char ch = '\\'
```

The other special codes are used in a similar manner.

Using Constant Values

Constants are identifiers that cannot change during execution of your program. A program can have constants of any of the five basic data types. C has three types of constants: integer constants, floating-point constants, and character constants.

To declare a constant, use the reserved word const, followed by the identifier, and then an assignment statement. Examples of constant declarations include the following:

```
const int speed = 75;
const float pi = 3.1415927;
const double diameter = 899.567;
const char ch = 'P';
```

Notice that the only difference between variable declarations and constant declarations is the reserved word const. All the constants are given a value that cannot change during the execution of a program. Remember that in earlier examples you could give a variable a beginning value, but that value could be changed during program execution.

Constants are similar to #define preprocessor directives, about which you learned earlier, but constants are easier to use when you are debugging. Using constants usually is better than using #define declarations, which are still around only because the original C language definition had no constant definition; therefore, programmers had no choice.

Constants cannot be changed during program execution. Listing 3.3 provides an example of using constants in the C programming language.

Listing 3.3   A Sample Constant Program

```
/************************************************
    CONSTS.C - Sample program that uses constants.
 ************************************************/

#include <stdio.h>

int main()
{
    const char letter = 'X';
    const float pi = 3.1415927;
    const int value = 12345;
```

```
    printf("The constants include:\n\
      character       = %c\n\
        floating point = %f\n\
        integer        = %d\n",
        letter, pi, value);

    return 0;
}
```

The first section of the program declares constant values, which then are displayed on-screen.

> **Note**
>
> Notice the use of the ending backslash in the first four lines to the `printf()` function. This notation tells the compiler to combine physical lines into one. In this program, the first four lines of the `printf()` function call appear to the compiler to be a single line.

Take a look at an example of a program that uses different types of variables and constants. In Chapter 2, "Your First Program," you learned how to declare and use a floating-point variable. The program in listing 3.4 uses character, integer, and floating-point variables to get input from the user and display the user's value.

Listing 3.4   A Program that Uses a Variety of Variables

```
/***********************************
  VARS.C - Program to show the use of
           variables in C.
***********************************/

#include <stdio.h>

int main()
{
    char letter;
    int number;
    float amount;
    const double pi = 3.1415927;

    printf("Enter a Character\n");
    scanf("%c", &letter);

    printf("Enter an Integer Number\n");
    scanf("%d", &number);

    printf("Enter a Floating-Point Number\n");
    scanf("%f", &amount);

    printf("\n\n");
```

(continues)

Listing 3.4 Continued

```
        printf("The character, 'letter' "
               "is equal to %c\n", letter);
        printf("The integer, 'number' "
               "is equal to %d\n", number);
        printf("The floating point, 'amount' "
               "is equal to %f\n", amount);
        printf("The double constant, 'pi' "
               "is equal to %f\n", pi);

        return 0;
    }
```

The program uses the `printf()` and `scanf()` functions to display output and get input from the user. A sample interaction with the user looks like this:

```
Enter a Character
p
Enter an Integer Number
24
Enter a Floating-Point Number
768.867

The character, 'letter' is equal to p
The integer, 'number' is equal to 24
The floating point, 'amount' is equal to 768.867000
The double constant, 'pi' is equal to 3.141593
```

The first part of the program prompts the user to enter three types of variables. The user must press the Enter key each time for the computer to store the value in the computer.

The second part of the program displays the values of the three variables that the user entered, along with the value of a floating-point constant declared at the beginning of the program.

Listing 3.4 is a simple example of using variables and constant values in programs. Throughout this book, you will see variables used; there is no getting away from them. A program without variables is like a sandwich without the filling.

Using Arrays

An *array* is a list (or table) of variables of a related type. The variables in an array have a common name. Each individual item in the array is accessed with an integer number called an *index*. Index values always are positive numbers.

Following are two rules for using and defining arrays:

■ You must specify the *size* of the array, or how many elements it will hold.

■ Arrays can have two or more dimensions; therefore, you also must specify the *number of dimensions* of the array.

The number of dimensions refers to how many index values are used to access variables in the array. A *one-dimensional array* has a single index value and is similar to a list of data. A *two-dimensional array* has two index values and can represent objects such as graph paper or worksheets with rows and columns. Figure 3.1 shows the concepts of one-dimensional and two-dimensional arrays.

One-Dimensional Arrays

The simplest type of array is the one-dimensional (or single-dimensional) array.

Arrays

The general format of a one-dimensional array is

```
datatype variablename[size];
```

wherein *datatype* declares the type of the array (int, char, double, and so on) of each element and *size* defines how many elements the array holds. The *variablename* is the identifier you give to the array.

The following line declares an integer array named table, which is four elements long:

```
int table[4];
```

To refer to the elements of the array, use the index value. All array elements are numbered starting at 0. If you create an array with four elements, the first element is numbered 0, and the last element is numbered 3. Following are the statements used to access the declared array elements:

```
table[0] = 1;
table[1] = 2;
table[2] = 3;
table[3] = 4;
```

The four variables—table[0], table[1], table[2], and table[3]— have a common name, so they are distinguished by the index value 0, 1, 2, or 3. You can assign a value to each of the four variables. In the preceding example, the numbers 1 through 4 have been assigned to the variables.

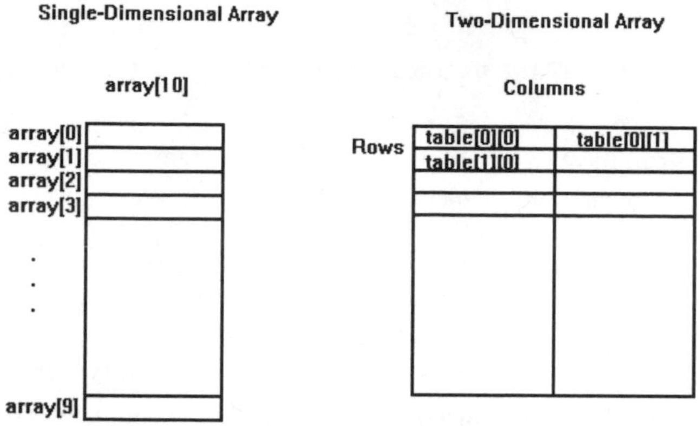

Fig. 3.1
One- and two-
dimensional
arrays.

Single-Dimensional Array

array[10]

array[0]
array[1]
array[2]
array[3]

.
.
.

array[9]

Two-Dimensional Array

Columns

Rows | table[0][0] | table[0][1]
table[1][0]

Bounds Checking

The C programming language performs no *bounds checking* on arrays—that is, there is no test to see whether the index value used in an array exceeds the actual size of the array. Nothing (except common sense) stops you from accessing elements at the end of an array that were not previously declared. As the programmer, you must ensure that all arrays are large enough to hold the data that the program will put in them. If you have any reason to believe that your program may be accessing array elements outside the declared array, you should add checks to the code to prevent such access.

Caution

C does not stop you from accessing elements at the end of an array that were not previously declared. If this happens, you will be assigning values to some other variable's memory space. Data entered with too large a subscript will simply be placed in memory outside the array.

You might be wondering why C does not provide bounds checking. The answer is that C was designed to compile programs that will execute as quickly as possible. Error checking slows the execution of a program. Therefore, it is the programmer's responsibility to prevent array overruns. Also, by not checking bounds, C gives the programmer more control of the variables in a program.

Initializing Arrays

Remember that you were able to declare a variable and initialize it to a specific value? You can perform the same initialization trick with arrays. To initialize array elements to specific values, specify initialization values at the time you declare the array. Following is an example:

```
int numbers[5] = { 1, 135, 10, 71, 23 };
```

The list of values is enclosed in braces, and the values are separated by commas.

Another form of array initialization enables you to omit the number that defines the size of the array. The compiler then counts the number of elements in the initialization list and creates an array with the appropriate size. For example, the following code

```
int numbers[] = { 1, 135, 10, 71, 23 };
```

creates the same-size array as the preceding one (with five elements), but it makes the compiler set the appropriate size of the array.

Multiple-Dimensional Arrays

The C programming language enables you to use multiple-dimensional arrays to reference more complex information. The simplest form of the multiple-dimensional array is the two-dimensional array. You can think of a two-dimensional array as being a list of one-dimensional arrays.

Two-dimensional arrays are defined in much the same manner as one-dimensional arrays, except that a separate pair of brackets is required for each index. Thus, a two-dimensional array requires two pairs of brackets. In general terms, a two-dimensional array is declared as follows:

```
int twodim[5][10];
```

This code declares a two-dimensional integer array named twodim, which you can think of as being a table with 5 rows and 10 columns.

Caution

The two-dimensional array declaration in C is a little different than in most computer languages. In Pascal, commas usually are used to separate array dimensions; in C, however, each dimension appears in its own set of brackets. Be sure that you don't try to refer to a two-dimensional array element as twodim[15,10], which will cause the compiler to issue an error message. The proper way to address this array element in C is twodim[15][10].

Initializing Multiple-Dimensional Arrays

Earlier in this chapter, you learned how to initialize one-dimensional arrays. You can initialize two-dimensional arrays in a similar manner. To initialize a sample two-dimensional array, use the following statement:

```
int initarr[3][5] =
   { { 45, 213, 78, 12, 98},
       { 12, 423, 27, 39, 76},
       { 19, 82,  47, 55, 100}  };
```

Again, as with one-dimensional arrays, the numbers in the brackets are optional. If you do not specify these numbers, C uses the number of provided elements as the size of the array.

String Variables

You might be wondering why a section about string variables is mixed with sections on arrays. The reason is that C has no intrinsic string-variable type. Instead, C programmers use character arrays.

In C, a string is characterized as being a number of character values terminated with a null value. A null is specified with the \0 escape sequence. It looks like two characters, but really is one.

> **Note**
>
> Because of the null terminator, you must declare character arrays to be one character longer than the largest string they hold.

The general definition of a character array looks like this:

```
char string[size];
```

In this example, *size* is the length of the string. Each character occupies one byte of memory. You always must make space for the terminating null character. If you know a string will be 10 characters long, you must define it as 11 characters long.

Initializing Strings

Just as numerical arrays can be initialized, so can character arrays. You can specify each character in the string like this:

```
char name[] = { 'P', 'r', 'o', 'g', 'r', 'a',
                'm', 's', '\0'  };
```

Alternatively, you can specify the characters as a single string, using quotation marks, as follows:

```
char name[] = "Programs";
```

These two lines mean the same thing to the compiler. Notice that it is easier to type a full string than individual characters separated with apostrophes and commas. When you declare the entire string at one time, you don't have to insert the terminating null character; the string initialization causes C to add the null character automatically.

An Array Example

The program in listing 3.5 uses two arrays. The program initializes an integer array with five values; it also uses a character array to store the name of the user. When the program is executed, it asks the user for her or his name. When the user's name has been entered, the program displays the name and the result of the average of the values inside the array.

Listing 3.5   A Program to Demonstrate Arrays in C

```
/************************************
   ARRAY.C - Program to show the use of
             arrays in C.
 ************************************/

#include <stdio.h>

int main()
{
   int data[5] = { 10, 50, 100, 150, 200 };
   char name[80];
   long avg;

   avg = ( data[0] + data[1] + data[2] +
           data[3] + data[4] ) / 5;

   printf("Please Enter Your Name: ");
   scanf("%s", &name);

   printf("\n");           /* Carriage Return */

   printf("Hey, %s, the average number is %d",
           name, avg);

   return 0;
}
```

When the program runs, it looks something like this:

```
Please Enter Your Name: Kevin

Hey, Kevin, the average number is 102
```

Later in this chapter, as you learn more about the C language, you will learn some ways to cycle through arrays that make them much easier to use. For the rest of this chapter, turn your focus to another important part of C programming: operators.

Using Operators

Operators work so closely with variables that just as it is hard to imagine a program without variables, it is difficult to create a useful C program that does not use operators. Remember that *operators* are words or symbols that cause a program to do something to its variables.

C uses several categories of operators. The rest of this section discusses how assignment operators, arithmetic operators, relational operators, unary operators, and logical operators are used to form expressions.

Assignment Operators

You saw the use of the assignment operator in Chapter 2, "Your First Program." An example follows:

```
int num;
num = 11;
```

The first statement declares an integer variable, giving it an identifier (num) and a type (int). The second statement uses the assignment operator (=) to assign the variable a value. The assignment operator has the same function as the := operator in Pascal and the = operator in BASIC.

Assignment expressions that use the = operator are written in this format:

```
identifier = expression;
```

In assignment expressions, *identifier* usually represents a variable, and *expression* represents a constant, a variable, or a more complex expression.

Arithmetic Operators

Chapter 2, "Your First Program," introduced arithmetic operators, which enable you to perform basic mathematical operations. C has five arithmetic operators: addition, subtraction, multiplication, division, and remainder. Table 3.2 describes these operators.

Table 3.2 Arithmetic Operators in C	
Operator	**Purpose**
+	Addition
-	Subtraction
*	Multiplication
/	Division
%	Remainder (modulus operator)

The C programming language uses the four arithmetic operators that are common in most other programming languages, including BASIC and Pascal. C also uses an operator that is not as common: the remainder operator.

The operands on which the arithmetic operators act must represent numeric values. Thus, the operands can be integer, floating-point, or character (because character variables actually are represented as integer quantities). Following the laws of mathematics, the division operator (/) requires that the second operand be nonzero.

Division of one integer value by another is called *integer division*. The % operator is the remainder after dividing integer values; this operator sometimes is referred to as the *modulus operator*. Integer division requires that both operands be integer variables as well as that the second operand be nonzero. The decimal portion of the quotient always is dropped in integer division.

In Chapter 2, listing 2.1 (FIRST.C) demonstrated the multiplication operator (*). Remember that the listing included a statement like this one:

```
area = PI * radius * radius;
```

This statement multiplied the value of the variable radius by itself and then multiplied it by the value defined by PI. The result is assigned to the variable area.

Following is another example of multiplication:

```
days = age * 365;
```

Similar to the preceding example, this one multiplies the value of the variable age (assumed to be in years) by the integer value 365 (the number of days in a year), thus informing a user how old (in days) he or she is. Both of the preceding examples use simple multiplication.

Some more examples follow:

```
result = 365/5;
total = 27 + 83;
value = 99 - previous;
```

These examples are basic, easy-to-understand mathematical equations. The C programming language, however, can handle more complex expressions easily. As an exercise, try to write a program that combines the arithmetic operators to create more complex expressions.

Relational Operators

The C programming language has six relational operators, which are listed in table 3.3.

Table 3.3	Relational Operators in C		
Operator	**Explanation**	**Example(s)**	**Description**
<	Less than	5 < 10	5 is less than 10
>	Greater than	10 > 5	10 is greater than 5
==	Equal to	10 == 10	10 is equal to 10
!=	Not equal to	9 != 10	9 is not equal to 10
<=	Less than or equal to	5 <= 5	5 is less than or equal to 5
		5 <= 10	5 is less than or equal to 10
>=	Greater than or equal to	10 >= 10	10 is greater than or equal to 10
		20 >= 10	20 is greater than or equal to 10

Relational operators compare two values. If the values compare correctly according to the relational operator, the expression is considered to be true; otherwise it is considered to be false. The resulting expressions represent an expression of type integer, because true is represented by the integer value 1 and false is represented by the integer value 0.

The expression 10 > 9 (10 is greater than 9), for example, results in a true value. The expression 9 > 10 (9 is greater than 10), however, is a false expression. Listing 3.6 provides an example of the relational operators.

Listing 3.6   Working with Relational Operators

```
/************************************************
  RELATION.C - Using relational operators.
 ************************************************/

#include <stdio.h>

int main()
{
   int i;

   i = 9;

   printf("i is equal to %d\n\n",i);

   printf("i < 5 is %d\n",   i <  5);   /* False */
   printf("i > 4 is %d\n",   i >  4);   /* True  */
   printf("i == 9 is %d\n",  i == 9);   /* True  */
```

```
    printf("i != 8 is %d\n",  i != 8);   /* True  */
    printf("i <= 7 is %d\n",  i <= 7);   /* False */
    printf("i >= 6 is %d\n",  i >= 6);   /* True  */

    return 0;
}
```

The program declares a variable and assigns a starting value to that variable; then the program carries out a series of relational tests. The output of the program looks similar to this:

```
i is equal to 9

i < 5 is 0
i > 4 is 1
i == 9 is 1
i != 8 is 1
i <= 7 is 0
i >= 6 is 1
```

Each printf() statement includes a relational operator and returns a value of 1 (true) or 0 (false). The tests in the sample program mimic the available relational operators.

Unary Operators

The C programming language includes some rather unusual unary operators. Although this section covers only two of C's unary operators, those operators are the most interesting ones. The unary operators act on a single operand to produce a new value.

The two unary operators covered in this section are the *increment operator* (++) and the *decrement operator* (--). The increment operator increases its operand by one, whereas the decrement operator decreases its operand by one. These two operators work only on a single operand.

An example follows:

```
int i;
i = 0;
++i;
--i;
```

This example causes the integer variable i to be incremented by one (in the third line) and decremented by one (in the fourth line). This code is equal to the following statements:

```
int i;
i = 0;
i = i + 1;
i = i - 1;
```

The increment and decrement operators are used in different ways, depending on whether the operator appears before or after the operand. If the operator precedes the operand (++i), the operand will be altered in value before it is used in the statement (this is called the *prefix operator*). If the operator follows the operand (i++), the value of the operand will be changed after the variable is used (this syntax is called the *postfix operator*).

At this point, it may not seem important whether the operand is altered before or after it is used. Listing 3.7, which demonstrates the increment operator with both prefix and postfix notation, should clear up the matter for you. Type and run the program now.

Listing 3.7   Decrement Operator Example

```
/*******************************************************
   UNARY.C - Shows the use of the decrement operator.
*******************************************************/

#include <stdio.h>

int main()
{
    int value;

    value = 10;

    printf("value = %d\n", value);
    printf("value = %d\n", --value);
    printf("value = %d\n", value);
    printf("value = %d\n", value--);
    printf("value = %d\n", value);

    return 0;
}
```

The program's output looks like this:

```
value = 10
value = 9
value = 9
value = 9
value = 8
```

The program declares an integer variable and assigns it a value of 10. The starting value of the variable is displayed in the first `printf()` statement. The next statement decrements the value of the variable and displays its output; the statement uses the prefix increment operator. The next line displays the new value of the variable (the same value as the one displayed in the preceding line).

Now use the postfix version of the increment operator. Notice that the printed output for the fourth line is the same as that for the preceding line.

You know that the variable was decremented, however, because the final value displayed is what you expect, due to the use of the postfix version of the increment operator.

This example illustrates the power of the decrement operator (and, indirectly, the increment operator). These operators give the programmer complete control of when the operator modifies the value and what value a program returns.

The increment and decrement unary operators are examples of operators in the C programming language that other programming languages just don't have. As you continue your exploration of C, you will discover more features that are not available in other programming languages.

Logical Operators

In addition to the relational and equality operators, C contains three logical operators, which are presented in table 3.4.

Table 3.4   Logical Operators in C

Operator	Description	Explanation
&&	AND	Result is true if both expressions are true
¦¦	OR	Result is true if either expression is true
!	NOT	Reverses the condition of the expression

The logical operators are rather unusual because they usually work on operands that also are logical expressions (although not always). The result of using logical operators on logical expressions is that simple statements are combined to create complex conditions.

To put this in the context of everyday living, you would call an expression such as "If it is sunny, I will go swimming" a simple expression. Another simple expression might be "If I have time, I will go swimming." You can combine these simple statements and say, "If I have time *and* if it is sunny, I will go swimming." This result is a complex statement.

Before looking at complex statements, you need to get an overall feel for the use of logical operators.

The logical AND and logical OR operators work on two operands to return a logical value based on the operands. The logical NOT operator works on a single operand. Tables 3.5, 3.6, and 3.7 show the results of the logical tests. Notice that every logical value is represented by either an *x* or *y* value. The result signifies how the logical operator is evaluated.

Table 3.5 Logical *AND* (&&) Truth Table		
x	**y**	**Result**
1	1	1 (true)
1	0	0 (false)
0	1	0 (false)
0	0	0 (false)

Table 3.6 Logical *OR* (¦¦) Truth Table		
x	**y**	**Result**
1	1	1 (true)
1	0	1 (true)
0	1	1 (true)
0	0	0 (false)

Table 3.7 Logical *NOT* (!) Truth Table	
x	**Result**
1	0 (false)
0	1 (true)

Following are several examples of logical operators:

```
1 && 1
0 ¦¦ 0
!1
```

The first statement is an example of the AND operator. As listed in table 3.5, this operator should return a value of 1. This is the only time that the AND logical operator returns a true value; at all other times, it returns a false value.

The second statement shows the use of the OR operator, which returns a false condition. This is the one condition for which the OR operator returns a false value; in all other cases in table 3.6, OR returns a true value.

The last statement demonstrates the NOT operator. It takes only one operator, and returns a logical expression that is the opposite of the one on which it operates.

Logical expressions are important to the way computers are used. The microprocessor uses only logical tests; fortunately, you do not always have to use them. C provides these expressions to give you close interaction with the microprocessor.

Listing 3.8 is an example of a program that uses complex logical statements. Type and execute the program now.

Listing 3.8   Examples of Complex Logical Statements

```
/**********************************************
   LOGIC.C - Tests the logical operators.
 **********************************************/

#include <stdio.h>

int main()
{
    int a,b;

    a = 1;
    b = 2;

    printf("Beginning values:\n");
    printf("a = %d\nb = %d\n\n", a,b);
    printf("Tests:\n");
    printf("a == 1 is %d\n", a == 1);    /* True */
    printf("b != 1 is %d\n", b != 1);    /* True */
    printf("Therefore, (a == 1) && (b != 1) is %d\n",
           ( a == 1 ) && ( b != 1 ) );
    return 0;
}
```

The program's output looks like this:

```
Beginning values:
a = 1
b = 2

Tests:
a == 1 is 1
b != 1 is 1
Therefore, (a == 1) && (b != 1) is 1
```

The program starts by assigning beginning values to two variables (a and b); it then displays the result of two simple statements. Finally, the program combines the simple statements into a complex one and displays the result.

Understanding Operator Precedence

When you were working with arithmetic operators, you used parentheses to force the compiler to evaluate things in a different order. It is appropriate, then, to ask how the compiler evaluates operators.

You must determine the order in which operators are applied. This order is specified by *operator precedence*, which is summarized in table 3.8. Operators with highest precedence (or those that are applied first) are at the top of the list; those with lower precedence appear farther down the list.

Table 3.8   Operator Precedence in C

Operator Type	Operators	Associativity
Unary	- -, ++	Right to left
Logical NOT	!	Right to left
Multiplication	*, /, %	Left to right
Addition	+, -	Left to right
Relational	<, <=, >, >=	Left to right
Relational (Equality)	==, !=	Left to right
Logical AND	&&	Left to right
Logical OR	¦¦	Left to right
Assignment	=	Right to left

Each group of operators in the table has a certain associativity (relationship to one another). The operators are evaluated from the left or from the right. The only time this table is used is when you mix operators of different types.

Note

Remember that you can use parentheses to override the precedence of any of the operators.

Summary

This chapter delved into the heart of C programming. You examined the basic C data types, learned about arrays, and learned what operators are and which ones are available in C. In Chapter 4, you will be introduced to the topics of keyboard input and video output.

In particular, this chapter covered the following topics:

- A *variable* is the name for a location in memory. When a programmer declares a variable, the variable must be given a name (or identifier) and a type. The name determines how you refer to the variable. The type of the variable refers to how much memory you set aside for the variable and the size of the information that the variable can hold.

- The C programming language has four basic *data types:* integer (`int`), floating-point (`float`), double-precision (`double`), and character (`char`).

- C uses three basic types of *floating-point numbers:* `float`, `double`, and `long double`. The difference between them is the magnitude of the largest and smallest number they can hold.

- *Constants* are identifiers that cannot be changed during program execution.

- *Arrays* are groups of similar or related variables that have a common name. Each element in an array is accessed with an index to the array. Arrays always start at index zero and go to one less than the length of the array.

- The C programming language performs no *bounds checking* on arrays—that is, there is no test to see whether the index value used in an array exceeds the actual size of the array. Nothing stops you from accessing elements at the end of an array that were not declared. It is your responsibility to make sure that the subscripts of an array do not go beyond the size of the array.

- In C, *string variables* actually are arrays of characters. The string must be terminated with a \0 escape character (null) to signify the end of the string.

- *Operators* are symbols that cause a program to do something to its variables.

- The *assignment operator* is used to assign the value of one identifier to another.

- The *arithmetic operators* in C include + (addition), - (subtraction), * (multiplication), / (division), and % (remainder).

- *Relational operators* compare two values. If the values compare correctly according to the relational operator, the expression is considered to be true (1); otherwise, the expression is considered to be false (0).

- *Unary operators*, which are unique to C, allow a variable to be incremented or decremented by 1.

- *Logical operators* work on two operands to return a logical value based on the operands. The C language includes the && (AND), ¦¦ (OR), and ! (NOT) logical operators.

- *Operator precedence* determines the order in which expressions are evaluated in C. Operators with the highest precedence are applied first. The order of precedence is listed in table 3.8.

Chapter 4

Keyboard Input and Video Output

C does not directly provide for input and output operations. Instead, input and output are accomplished through the use of *library functions* (standard functions included with the compiler). Most C compilers define a complete set of input and output functions that handle I/O operations.

To access an I/O function from anywhere in a program, enter the function name, followed by a list of arguments in parentheses. The arguments represent data items that are sent to the function. Some I/O functions do not require arguments, but empty parentheses still must appear in the function call.

To access the input/output functions, your compiler usually provides a collection of header files. These files contain the necessary information to support the various types of I/O functions. As a rule, the header file required by the standard group of input/output library functions is STDIO.H. This file is used in all programs that interact with the user.

Character I/O

The C input and output functions use a type of buffered input. *Buffered input* is the result of collecting and storing the characters you typed in an area of temporary memory called a *buffer*. When you finish entering the text, you press the Enter key, making the block of characters available to the input routine. The characters are not sent to the input routine (and, therefore, are not available to your program) until you press Enter.

A program that echoes input characters immediately uses a form of *unbuffered input*, which means that the characters entered by the user are available to your program immediately. For example, if typing the letter *A* causes an action to take place immediately, you have witnessed unbuffered input. If, on the other hand, you type the letter *A* and then must press the Enter key to force the input to be accepted, you are using a form of buffered input.

There are several advantages of using buffered input. First, if you type something incorrectly, you can use the Backspace key to correct your mistake. When you finally press the Enter key, your program receives the corrected version of the input. Furthermore, it is less time-consuming to transmit characters as a single block than to send them one at a time.

Unbuffered input is desirable for real-time or interactive applications. If you are writing a fast-paced, action-packed arcade game, you would not want to force the user to press the Enter key every time keyboard input is expected. In a spreadsheet program, as another example, each command should execute as soon as the user presses a key for best user-program interaction. For example, the user should be able to press F9 to have the spreadsheet calculated, rather than pressing F9 and Enter.

Thus, both buffered and unbuffered input have their places. You might wonder which type of buffering to use in your program. As the examples illustrate, it usually depends on what type of program you are writing. It also depends on the type of system on which you are running your program.

Note

The ANSI C specification does not include functions for unbuffered keyboard input. Most C compilers, however, have extended the standard runtime library to include unbuffered input.

Buffered Character I/O

You can input single characters with the C library function `getchar()`. The `getchar()` function is part of the standard group of I/O library routines. Therefore, the compiler requires the use of the STDIO.H header file for prototype information. The `getchar()` function returns a single character from the standard input device (usually the keyboard). The function does not require any arguments, although a pair of empty parentheses must follow the function name.

Buffered Character I/O

In general, the `getchar()` function is written as follows:

```
character_variable = getchar();
```

`character_variable` refers to some previously declared character variable (defined by the programmer before using the variable). Notice that `getchar()` reads from the standard input device and is buffered. The function does not return a value until you press Enter, as follows:

```
char c;       /* declare variable */
c = getch(); /* get character value */
```

The counterpart to the `getchar()` function is the `putchar()` function, which displays a single character on the video display. The `putchar()` function is part of the standard C language I/O library. The function outputs a single character to the standard output device (the video display). The character to be displayed is represented as a character type variable. The character is expressed as an argument to the function, enclosed in parentheses. In general, a reference to the `putchar()` function is as follows:

```
putchar(character_variable);
```

`character_variable` refers to some previously declared character variable. The following code shows how `putchar()` is used:

```
char c = 'X'; /* declare variable */
putchar(c);   /* display variable */
```

Listing 4.1 shows how to use the `getchar()` and `putchar()` functions. The program waits for you to press a key and then displays that key press on-screen.

Listing 4.1   A Character I/O Example

```
/**************************************************
   CHARIO.C - Inputting and outputting a character
              variable.
 **************************************************/

#include <stdio.h>

int main()
{
   char c;

   c = getchar();
   putchar(c);

   return 0;
}
```

Notice the use of the STDIO.H header file at the beginning of the program. This file defines standard input and output for the C language (it is required in almost every program). As your programs become longer, you may need several header files at the beginning.

Unbuffered Character I/O

Both the Borland and Microsoft compilers on the PC have unbuffered character I/O routines. The getch() function reads a character from the keyboard without any buffering. Furthermore, the character that the user entered is not displayed on-screen.

To get unbuffered input from the keyboard and display it on-screen at the same time, use the getche() function (the *e* stands for echo).

Unbuffered Character I/O

In general, these functions are written as follows:

```
character_variable = getch();
```

and

```
character_variable = getche();
```

`character_variable` refers to some previously declared character variable and contains the character that the user entered. The following code lines show getch() and getche() in action:

```
char c;
c = getch();
c = getche();
```

These two functions don't buffer their input—in other words, the function returns immediately when the user presses the appropriate key. The only difference between getch() and getche() is that getche() echoes the character to the video display (hence, the *e* in its name), whereas getch() does not.

Formatted I/O

Before you can start using the formatted keyboard and screen I/O functions, you have to know how C handles input, output, and data. C uses *streams* to represent the data that moves in and out of a program. C streams enable you to use your computer's I/O devices without worrying about low-level control of your computer. You perform most types of I/O with the system through streams. In Chapter 11, "Working with Files," you learn how disk files are accessed through streams.

Streams are a portable way to handle input/output tasks. They are used for all types of input and output, including manipulation of data files. The powerful aspect of using streams with C is that the code is transferable to different compilers on different computer platforms.

This feature might not seem powerful if you write programs for only one computer system, but large-system houses use C entirely for this benefit. When you want to write a program for a different computer, you can simply transfer the C code to the new system and make small changes. Rewriting the program for each platform would take much more time and energy.

Most C compilers provide several predefined streams for use in your programs. Whenever you write a C program, you automatically have access to the following standard streams:

Stream Name	Description	Device
stdin	Input stream	Keyboard
stdout	Output stream	Video display
stdprn	Printer stream	Printer port
stdaux	Auxiliary output	Serial port
stderr	Error stream	Video display

Using these standard streams is easy because you do not have to perform any extra housekeeping chores (as you must when you access disk files). C automatically opens the standard streams so that they are available when your program executes.

Formatted I/O Functions

In Chapter 1, "C Programming Basics," you were exposed (briefly) to the two basic formatted I/O functions: the scanf() and printf() functions. *Formatted input and output* refers to the capability to input data from the user in a format with which you are familiar. Suppose that you are familiar with the floating-point number 3.1415 but not with the binary codes that store the number in memory. Formatted I/O basically is an easier way for you to access data.

The printf() and scanf() functions work with formatted data. The scanf() function gets input from the user, whereas the printf() function displays output for the user. When you use either function, specify the type of data with which you are working.

Both printf() and scanf() work with C's basic data types. For example, you can use these functions to input integer data just as easily as you can use them to input floating-point data or character data.

The *printf()* Function

The printf() function consists of two main parts: a format string and a variable argument list. The format string specifies what type of data is output. The variable argument list supplies that data. Table 4.1 is a list of valid format specifiers for the printf() function.

Output with *printf()*

In general terms, the printf() function is accessed as follows:

```
printf("control string", arg1, arg2, ..., argx);
```

control string refers to a string that contains formatting information, and *arg1, arg2, ..., argx* are arguments that represent the individual output data items. The arguments can be written as constants, single variable names, or more complex expressions.

The control string comprises individual groups of characters, with one character group for each output data item. Each character group must begin with the percent sign (%). The combination of a character group with the percent sign is known as a *format specifier*. The following code shows how to output text with printf():

```
int x = 999;
printf("Now is the time");
printf("An integer is %d", 123);
printf("An integer variable is %d", x);
```

The first line displays the entire string passed to it on the video display. The second line displays an integer constant, and the third line displays an integer variable.

Table 4.1   Format Specifiers for the *printf()* Function

Format Specifier	Output Type
%d	Signed decimal integer
%f	Floating-point
%e	Floating-point with exponential notation
%x	Unsigned hexadecimal integer

Format Specifier	Output Type
%o	Unsigned octal integer
%c	Character
%s	String

The simplest form of the printf() function is one without the variable argument list. The variable argument list for the printf() function is not required; it is perfectly legal to use the function without specifying the argument list. For example, the following line of code simply uses the printf() function to print a message on-screen:

```
printf("This will be displayed on the screen\n");
```

Caution

If you use format specifiers, you must make sure that the conversion specifications match the variables you provide. A mismatch between the format string and the variable argument list causes strange program behavior.

Following is a line of code that uses a format specifier:

```
printf("The value is %d", result);
```

When the compiler interprets this line, it replaces the value of the variable result with the format specifier. If the value of the variable result is 5, for example, the output would look like this:

```
The value is 5
```

The compiler automatically replaces the %d with the value of result.

You can insert many special escape codes into a control string to control output. These codes enable you to output characters that do not appear on your keyboard. Table 4.2 lists the special escape codes that you can use in a string.

Table 4.2 Special Escape Sequences	
Code	**Description**
\\	Backslash
\b	Backspace
\r	Carriage return

(continues)

Table 4.2	**Continued**
Code	**Description**
\ "	Double quotations
\f	Formfeed
\n	Newline
\0	Null value
\ '	Single quotation
\t	Tab
\v	Vertical tab
\a	Bell
\ooo	ASCII character in octal
\x###	Hex character
\?	Question mark

The most frequently used control sequence is the \n or newline escape sequence, which separates lines of output. In the following code fragment, \n is used to separate output lines between subsequent printf() calls:

```
printf("One\nTwo\nThree");
```

This line appears on-screen as follows:

```
One
Two
Three
```

The \n code instructs the printf() function to separate the output lines by inserting a carriage return and line feed every time the \n code is located in the control string.

You also can pass values to the printf() function in hexadecimal. As you know, every character is represented in the computer by an ASCII (American Standard Code for Information and Interchange) value. You can use the \xddd escape sequence to specify a hex value to the printf() function. Listing 4.2 gives an example.

Listing 4.2   Displaying Hex Values with *printf()*

```
/**************************************************
   HEX.C - Displaying hex values.
 **************************************************/
```

```
#include <stdio.h>

int main()
{
    printf("\x048\x065\x06c\x06c\x06f\x02c\x020");
    printf("\x057\x06f\x072\x06c\x064\x021\n");
    printf("\n");
    return 0;
}
```

The output of listing 4.2 looks like this:

```
Hello, World!
```

You never would guess the output by examining the code, because you specified each letter in the string `"Hello World!"` with its ASCII code in hex. You probably will not use this method of displaying characters very often, but it comes in handy when you need to display some special characters.

Listing 4.3 shows another example of using the `printf()` function in a program. The program, PRINTF.C, asks the user to enter a number, in inches. The program then converts the value to centimeters and displays the result on-screen.

Listing 4.3   An Inches-to-Centimeters Conversion Program

```
/***************************************************
    PRINTF.C - Sample program showing use of the
               printf() function.
 ***************************************************/

#include <stdio.h>

int main()
{
    float inches, cent;
                    /* Variable declarations */

    printf("How many inches? ");
    scanf("%f", &inches);
                    /* Get input from user */
    cent = inches * 2.54;
                    /* Calculation */
    printf("%.2f Inches is %.2f Centimeters\n", inches, cent);

    return 0;
}
```

The following is a sample execution of the PRINTF.C program:

```
How many inches? 4.5

4.50 Inches is 11.43 Centimeters
```

The screen shows the conversion of 4.5 inches to 11.43 centimeters. The program uses the scanf() function to prompt the user for the number of inches (you will learn about the scanf() function later in this chapter) and then performs the calculation. Finally, the program uses the printf() function to demonstrate the use of the %f format specifier to display the values. The format characters in these lines look a little different from those in table 4.2 because these use a field-width specifier to format the data, as follows:

```
printf("%.2f Inches is %.2f Centimeters\n", inches, cent);
```

The entered number, 4.5, was later displayed as 4.50. The %.2f format specifier instructs the printf() function to use the format specifier for floating-point numbers. A .2 was placed between the % and the f in the preceding example to further customize the output. This specification enables the programmer to control how many characters are printed after the decimal point. In this example, two characters are displayed, so 4.5 was displayed as 4.50.

The programmer also can control how many spaces are printed before the decimal point. A digit preceding the decimal point determines the space created to hold the number when it is displayed. This procedure is helpful in lining up tables of numbers with a decimal point. Here is a code example:

```
printf("%6.2f%6.2f%6.2f\n", 1.6, 49.01, 1600.2);
printf("%6.2f%6.2f%6.2f\n", 1600.2, 1.6, 49.01);
```

The following lines are the result of this function:

```
   1.60    49.01  1600.2
1600.20     1.6    49.01
```

Notice how the decimal points are aligned. Although the format specifiers may be confusing, the output is formatted nicely.

Next, study listing 4.4 to learn the effect of the field-width modifiers on printing output.

Listing 4.4   An Example of Field-Width Specifiers

```
/*********************************************
  WIDTHSP.C - Example of width specifiers.
*********************************************/

#include <stdio.h>

int main()
{
   const int value = 768;

   printf("[%d]\n", value);
   printf("[%2d]\n", value);
   printf("[%5d]\n", value);
```

```
    printf("[%10d]\n", value);

    return 0;
}
```

The program uses the brackets to show where each field begins and ends.
The output of the program looks like this:

```
[768]
[768]
[  768]
[      768]
```

The first conversion specification is %d with no width specifier. This specification produces a field with the default width as the size of the integer being
printed. The second width specification is %2d. This specification produces a
field width three digits long; the field is automatically expanded to fit the
number.

The next conversion specification is %5d, which produces a field five digits
long. Notice that there are three spaces for the number and two additional
blank spaces. The final specification, %10d, produces a field 10 spaces wide.

You also can specify the maximum number of decimal places for a floating-
point value, or the maximum number of characters for a string. This specification is known as the *field precision*. The precision is an unsigned integer
that is preceded by a decimal place.

Sometimes, a floating-point number is rounded if it must be shortened to
conform to a precision specification. Listing 4.5 illustrates the use of the precision feature with floating-point numbers.

Listing 4.5   An Example of Precision Specification with *printf()*

```
/**************************************************
   PRECISE.C - Using precision with printf().
**************************************************/

#include <stdio.h>

int main()
{
   float y = 123.456;

   printf("%7f %7.3f %7.1f\n", y, y, y);
   printf("%12e %12.5e %12.3e", y, y, y);

   return 0;
}
```

When the program is executed, the following output is generated:

```
123.456001 123.456    123.5
1.23456e+002 123456e+002    1.235e+002
```

The first line is produced by using the %f format specifier. Notice the rounding that occurs in the third value (123.5) because of the single-decimal-place precision specification. You also can see the leading blanks that were added as a result of the seven-character width specifier.

The second line uses the %e format specifier. You can see the use of exponential notation used to display the value. Again, the third number is rounded to conform to the specified precision.

A minimum-field-width specification is not necessary with the precision specification. You can specify the precision without the minimum field width, but a decimal point still must precede the precision.

In summary, the format specifier in the printf() function determines the interpretation of a variable's type, the width of the field, the number of decimal places printed, and the justification.

The *scanf()* Function

You can enter data into the computer from a standard input device by means of the library function scanf(). You can use this function to enter any combination of numerical values and single characters. The function returns the number of data items that were entered correctly.

Using the scanf() function to get data is an example of buffered input; the user must press Enter or Return after entering the data.

Input with *scanf()*

In general, the scanf() function has the following parameters:

scanf(*control string*, *arg1*, *arg2*, ..., *argx*);

control string refers to a string containing certain required formatting information, and *arg1*, *arg2*, ..., *argx* are arguments that represent the individual data items. Actually, the arguments represent pointers that indicate the addresses of the data items in the computer's memory.

The control string comprises individual groups of characters, with one character group for each input data item. Each character group must begin with a percent sign (%). In its simplest form, a single character group consists of the percent sign, followed by a conversion character that indicates the type of the corresponding data item.

The multiple-character groups in the control string can be adjacent, or they can be separated by white-space characters (blank spaces, tabs, or carriage returns). If the control string contains any blanks or tabs, they are ignored.

If white-space characters are used to separate multiple-character groups in the control string, all consecutive white-space characters in the input data are read but ignored. The use of blank spaces as character-group separators is common. Table 4.3 lists the scanf() conversion codes. The following code shows scanf() in action:

```
int x;
scanf("%d",&x);
```

Caution

Remember that scanf() parameters are pointers, whereas printf() parameters are real values, not pointers. Confusing these two can cause unexpected results—your program probably will compile, and your system probably will crash!

Table 4.3 *scanf() Conversion Codes*

Character	Description
%c	Single character
%d	Signed decimal integer
%e	Floating-point value in exponential format
%f	Floating-point value
%h	Short integer
%i	Integer
%o	Octal integer
%s	String of characters
%u	Unsigned decimal integer
%x	Hexadecimal integer

Listing 4.6 shows the scanf() function in action.

Listing 4.6 A Sample *scanf()* Program

```
/**************************************************
   SCANF.C - Sample program showing use of scanf()
             function.
 **************************************************/

#include <stdio.h>

int main()
{
   float age, days;

   printf("How many years old are you? ");
   scanf("%f", &age);
   days = age * 365;
   printf("\nYou are %.1f days old.\n", days);

   return 0;
}
```

The program prompts the user for his or her age (in years) and then converts the number of years to days by multiplying by 365 (the program does not check for leap years) and displaying the person's age in days. Program execution looks something like this:

```
How many years old are you? 55
You are 20075.0 days old.
```

As you can see, the format specifiers for the scanf() function look much like those for the printf() function. As with printf(), the first argument is a string that contains the format specifiers. In this case, there is only one (%f). The following parameters are variable names. This program introduces a new symbol—the ampersand (&)—added to the beginning of variable arguments.

> **Note**
>
> As mentioned earlier, the arguments of the scanf() function actually are the addresses of variables, rather than the actual variables. The & character returns the actual memory address of a variable. This is an important concept in C programming; you learn about it in more detail in Chapter 9, "Using Pointers."

Remember that you should use an ampersand (&) before the variable name when calling to scanf(). By far the most common error is writing the following

```
scanf("%d", i);
```

rather than

```
scanf("%d", &i);
```

The compiler generally does not detect this error, and no warning message is displayed. This error causes your program to operate improperly and usually is a headache to track down.

By specifying an ampersand, you actually tell the compiler to pass the address of the variable to the function, rather than the value of the variable. The function then accesses the value of the variable by accessing the memory location directly.

Suppose that you want to query the user for more than one data item. You would use the program shown in listing 4.7.

Listing 4.7 Entering Multiple Data Items with *scanf()*

```
/***************************************************
   SCANF2.C - Inputting multiple items with scanf().
 ***************************************************/

#include <stdio.h>

int main()
{
  char name[20];
  int part;
  float cost;

  printf("Please enter name, part number, and cost\n");

  scanf("%s %d %f", &name, &part, &cost);

  printf("Name is: %s\n"
         "Part is: %d\n"
         "Cost is: %f\n",
           name, part, cost);

  return 0;
}
```

Following is a sample interaction with the user:

```
Please enter name, part number, and cost
GinsuKnife 1234 19.95
Name is: GinsuKnife
Part is: 1234
Cost is: 19.950000
```

Notice that the user must separate the multiple data items with white-space characters (Space, Tab, or Enter). You can see that the data items can continue to two or more lines, because Enter is considered to be a white-space character.

The individual data elements can also be entered as

```
GinsuKnife
1234
19.95
```

or as

```
GinsuKnife
1234 <tab> 19.95
```

whereby <tab> represents the user pressing the Tab key. The same information can even be input as follows:

```
GinsuKnife <tab> 1234 <tab> 19.95
```

I think you get the point. Because of this procedure, you cannot enter a string containing spaces in the same way. You have to use a string input function (as you will learn later in this chapter).

As a programming technique, you can see in the second call to `printf()` that a long string can be separated on several lines by putting quotations around the string. The line in question is

```
printf("Name is: %s\n"
"Part is: %d\n"
"Cost is: %f\n",
name, part, cost);
```

This same line can be entered this way:

```
printf("Name is: %s\nPart is: %d\nCost is: %f\n", name, part, cost);
```

Although the second form is acceptable, it is much easier for the programmer to read the first form. Highly readable code always is desirable.

String I/O Functions

Two important functions facilitate the transfer of strings between the computer and the standard I/O devices: the `gets()` and `puts()` functions. Their names represent *get string* and *put string,* which is exactly what the functions do.

Each function takes a single argument, which must be a character array (a string). The character array for the `puts()` function can include alphabetic, numeric, and any other special characters you might want to display.

String I/O with *gets( )* and *puts( )*

The `gets()` and `puts()` functions offer an alternative to the use of the `scanf()` and `printf()` functions for reading and displaying strings. The functions are declared like this:

```
gets(string)
```

and

```
puts(string)
```

The placeholder, *string*, represents any string variable. The following lines show an example of `gets()` and `puts()` in action:

```
char str[255];
char msg[] = "This is a message";
gets(str);  /* get string from the user */
puts(msg);  /* display the message*/
```

Listing 4.8 shows how the `gets()` and `puts()` functions operate. The program reads a line of text into the computer and then writes it to the screen in its original form.

Listing 4.8   Reading and Writing a Line of Text

```
/****************************************************
   STRINGIO.C - Example of string I/O functions.
****************************************************/

#include <stdio.h>

int main()
{
   char text[255];

   puts("Enter a line of text\n");
   gets(text);

   puts("\n\nText Entered: ");
   puts(text);

   return 0;
}
```

Following is a sample interaction with the program:

```
Enter a line of text
a crash course in c taught me

Text Entered:
a crash course in c taught me
```

The program uses the puts() and gets() functions to write text to the display and to get character input from the user.

> **Caution**
>
> Make sure that the array you create is large enough to hold the string that is to be entered. If the array is not large enough, a memory overwrite could occur, because the compiler does not do any bounds checking for arrays.

Summary

In this chapter, you studied fundamental input and output operations. The chapter focused on the interaction between the computer and the monitor. In particular, the chapter covered the following important points:

- The C language does not directly provide for input and output operations.

- Library functions must be used to access any type of I/O device, including the keyboard, the video display, the parallel printer port, the serial port, and any other I/O devices on your computer system.

- There are two types of input: *buffered* and *unbuffered*. Characters typed by the user that are stored in a temporary storage place until the user presses Enter are buffered input. Unbuffered input is sent, character by character, to the program as it is typed.

- C compilers provide several functions that perform character input and output.

- You learned how to get a single character from the user and display it on-screen with the getchar() and the putchar() functions.

- The C language declares several predefined streams for use in your programs. These streams give you automatic access to the keyboard, the video display, the printer port, the serial port, and a standard error stream that usually is routed to the video display.

- You use the scanf() function to input formatted data. This function enables you to specify the type and format of data to be input. The function expects you to supply a format string argument that specifies the data types to input; you also must supply a list of addresses that indicate where input data is to be stored.

■ You use the printf() function to output formatted data. This function enables you to specify the type and format of data to be output. The printf() function expects you to supply a format string argument that specifies the data types to output; you also must supply a list of variables to be output.

Chapter 5

Programs that Make Decisions

The essence of any computer program is the decisions it can make and act on. Every day, humans must make decisions based on certain facts and then act appropriately. For example, if somebody knocks on the front door, you look to see who it is. If it is a friend, you will ask him or her in for a cup of coffee. However, if you see the newspaper carrier, you will get your wallet so you can pay the monthly newspaper bill.

The same sort of decision-making process occurs in computer programs. The program tests conditions and responds to stimuli depending on the results of the tests. Any computer program must make decisions to be useful. The *conditional statements* discussed in this chapter enable a program to make decisions and act on them.

The C programming language has three major decision-making statements: the if statement, the if...else statement, and the switch statement. Also, the break statement allows the decision-making statements to have more flexibility. This chapter examines the ways C uses these decision-making statements.

The *if* Statement

When deciding which statements to execute, the computer considers all the current conditions of your program. The if statement is the basic decision-making statement in C.

The Simple *if* Statement

The general form of the `if` statement is

```
if (expression)
    statement;
```

The `if` statement enables you to test an expression and act according to how the expression is evaluated. If *expression* evaluates to true (1), the computer executes the statement that follows. However, if *expression* evaluates false (0), `statement` is not executed. The *expression* part of the `if` statement is a relational test—covered in Chapter 3, "Variables and Operators."

If you have used another programming language such as Pascal or BASIC, you will notice that the `if` statement in C does not use the `then` keyword. If you try to slip it in, your C compiler will correct you with the message `"undefined symbol 'then'"`. It then forces you to remove the undefined symbol before it compiles your program. The C language does not use the `then` keyword, to keep code notation lean and to the point.

For example, consider listing 5.1, which plays a version of a guess-the-number game. You are prompted to enter a number. The program uses the equality operator (==) to determine whether your guess matches the constant secretnumber declared in the program. If you enter the right number, the program displays the message `"You guessed it!"`. If you do not enter the correct number, the program displays nothing.

Listing 5.1   Guess the Number

```c
/****************************************************
    IF1.C - Sample program to demonstrate the
            if statement.
****************************************************/

#include <stdio.h>

int main()
{
    const int secretnumber = 21;
    int number;

    printf("Enter a number and try to "
           "guess the one "
           "I am thinking of: ");

    scanf("%d", &number);
```

```
    if (number == secretnumber)
        printf("\nYou guessed it!\n");

    return 0;
}
```

The `if` statement also can be displayed on one line, like this:

```
if(number == secretnumber) printf("\nYou guessed it!");
```

Splitting the statement into two lines makes it easier for people to read and understand.

When typing the listing, be careful not to type too many semicolons at the end of the line. Especially notice the line that begins with the `if` statement. It does not end with a semicolon, as lines usually do. The reason the `if` statement does not contain an ending semicolon is because the line following it is actually part of the statement. If you add an extra semicolon, such as

```
if(number == secretnumber);
    printf("\nYou guessed it!");
```

the `printf()` function is executed every time the program runs, regardless of whether the variable named `number` is equal to the constant `secretnumber`. The terminating semicolon in the `if` statement informs the compiler that the conditional statement is complete; the next `printf()` statement is executed like a regular statement. This conventional notation causes beginning C programmers to pull their hair out when they find the problem after hunting laboriously through the program for an error.

Note

The `if` statement is not generally a true statement by itself—in the simple `if` statement in listing 5.1, the `if` portion, (`if(number == secretnumber)`), is simply a clause of the rest of the statement, (`printf("\nYou guessed it!");`).

Using Program Blocks with the *if* Statement

The body of the `if` statement can consist of a single statement followed by a semicolon (as was demonstrated earlier) or by a number of statements surrounded by braces.

The Block *if* Statement

The modified form of the if statement that executes a block of statements follows:

```
if (expression)
{
statement1;
statement2;
.
.
.
statementX;
}
```

The set of braces surround the multiple statements if the expression evaluates to true. There is no limit to the number of statements you can include inside an if statement when you use braces. It is important to always include the pair of matching braces. If you forget to include one brace, the compiler gets confused quickly.

What follows is listing 5.2, which is a version of listing 5.1, rewritten to display several lines of congratulations to the player who guesses the correct number.

Listing 5.2   Using Program Blocks in an *if* Statement

```c
/*****************************************************
   CONGRAT.C - Guess the number with congratulations.
*****************************************************/

#include <stdio.h>

int main()
{
   const int secretnumber = 21;
   int number;

   printf("Enter a number and try "
           "to guess the one "
           "I am thinking of: ");

   scanf("%d", &number);

   if(number == secretnumber)
   {
      printf("\nYou guessed it!\n");
      printf("You must have special intelligence.\n");
      printf("Congratulations to you!\n");
   }

   return 0;
}
```

When CONGRAT.C is executed, the dialog with the user looks something like this:

```
Enter a number and try to guess
the one I am thinking of: 21

You guessed it!
You must have special intelligence.
Congratulations to you!
```

The multiple statements in the block are each terminated with a semicolon. The entire block is surrounded with braces. Using program blocks in an `if` statement allows the program to be more complex. This leads you to the next subject, that of nested `if` statements.

Nested *if* Statements

A nested `if` statement is an `if` statement that is included inside another `if` statement.

The Nested *if* Statement

The general format for the nested if statement is

```
if (expression)
if (another expression)
statement;
```

You will see that the second `if` statement is actually part of the body of the first `if` statement. The inner `if` statement is not executed unless the outer one evaluates to true. The *statement* is not executed unless both `if` statements evaluate to true.

Listing 5.3 shows how to use nested `if` statements. This is a modification of the original guess-a-number program. This time, if you don't guess the correct number, the program informs you whether you guessed too high or too low.

Listing 5.3   Using Nested *if* Statements

```
/*********************************************
   IF2.C - Example of nested if statements.
*********************************************/

#include <stdio.h>

int main()
{
   const int secretnumber = 21;
   int number;

   printf("Enter a number and try "
```

(continues)

Listing 5.3 Continued

```
                "to guess the one "
                "I am thinking of: ");

    scanf("%d", &number);

    if(number == secretnumber)
       printf("\nYou guessed it!");

    if(number != secretnumber)
    {
       printf("Sorry, you didn't guess it...\n");

       if (number > secretnumber)
            printf("You guessed too high\n");

       if (number < secretnumber)
          printf("You guessed too low\n");
    }

    return 0;
}
```

The program checks whether the number the player guessed is not equal (using the != operator) to secretnumber. If it is not, it checks whether the number is greater than or less than secretnumber. A message is then displayed depending on whether the number is greater than or less than secretnumber.

The *if...else* Statement

The if statement by itself is a powerful part of the C programming language that you can use to test expressions and take an appropriate action depending on the expression tested. The if statement executes a statement or group of statements when an expression evaluates to true. It does not take any action if the expression is false. This is where the if...else statement comes into action. The if...else statement allows a program to take a separate action if the expression does not evaluate to true.

The *if...else* Statement

The if...else statement is similar to the if statement. It adds an additional set of instructions, as follows:

```
    if (expression)
      statement1;
    else
      statement2;
```

The first two lines are the same as the original if statement. The else keyword signifies the statement to be executed if the expression does not evaluate to true.

To demonstrate the added power of the `if...else` statement, you can rewrite the number-guessing program, as shown in listing 5.4.

Listing 5.4   A Sample *if...else* Program

```
/**********************************************
   IFELSE.C - Rewritten number guessing game.
 **********************************************/

#include <stdio.h>

int main()
{
   const int secretnumber = 24;
   int number;

   printf("Enter a number and "
           "try to guess the "
           "one I am thinking of: ");
   scanf("%d", &number);

   if(number == secretnumber)
     printf("\nYou guessed it!\n");
   else
     printf("\nSorry, you didn't guess it\n");

   return 0;
}
```

See how the `if...else` statement simplifies the program? This program has a single `if...else` group of statements that either displays the message "You guessed it!" if you entered the correct number, or displays "Sorry, you didn't guess it" if the number was not equal to `secretnumber`.

All along, the example programs have tested different variables. You can also test a function because, as you will learn, functions return values. The following example, listing 5.5, tests the result of the `getchar()` function and displays a value depending on what the user enters.

Listing 5.5   A Program that Uses a Function as an Expression

```
/**************************************************
   IFELSE2.C - Sample program to use the result of
               a function call instead of testing
               an expression.
 **************************************************/

#include <stdio.h>
#include <ctype.h>

int main()
{
   printf("Type a key on the keyboard: ");
```

(continues)

Listing 5.5 Continued

```
    if ( toupper(getchar()) == 'Y')
        printf("\nYou pressed the Y key");
    else
        printf("\nYou did not press the Y key");

    return 0;
}
```

This example starts to show some of the power of the C programming language in testing the result of a function in an if...else statement. Notice the new function, toupper(), which converts a character to uppercase. It is defined in the CTYPE.H header file.

The if statement gets a character from the keyboard with a call to the getchar() function. It then converts that character to uppercase with the toupper() function and determines whether the character is equal to the letter *Y*. If the user typed the *Y* character (upper- or lowercase), the program makes the user aware of it. Otherwise, a message is displayed that informs the user that he or she did not press the *Y* key.

Nested *if...else* Statements

The if...else statement can be nested in the same manner as the if statement. However, you have to be careful because nested if...else statements can be ambiguous. For example, consider the program IFELSE3.C in listing 5.6.

Listing 5.6 A Nested *if...else* Example Program

```
/*********************************************
   IFELSE3.C - Nested if...else statements
*********************************************/

#include <stdio.h>

int main()
{
    int temp;

    printf("Please enter the current "
            "temperature\n");

    scanf("%d", &temp);

    if (temp < 85)
        if (temp > 65)
            printf("Sounds pretty comfortable.\n");
        else
            printf("Sort of chilly right now.\n");
```

```
    else
        printf("It is hot right now.\n");

    return 0;
}
```

The program nests two `if...else` statements. It asks the user to enter the current room temperature. If the temperature is less than 85, the program falls to the second `if` statement and checks whether the room temperature is greater than 65. If this is true (in which case the number the user entered is between 65 and 85), the program then displays a message `"Sounds pretty comfortable"`.

If the number is less than 65, the program displays the message `"Sort of chilly right now"`. Finally, if the number is greater than 85, the program falls to the final `else` statement, causing the computer to display the message `"It is hot right now"`.

Be careful when using nested `if` statements. For example, suppose you re-wrote the code to look like this:

```
if (temp < 85)
    if (temp > 65)
        printf("Sounds pretty comfortable.\n");
else
        printf("Sort of chilly right now.\n");
    else
    printf("It is hot right now.\n");
```

The actual code did not change; it is only formatted differently. It now seems that the first `else` statement belongs to the first `if` statement. However, the compiler still interprets the code in the same way. This inconsistency leads to problems that are difficult to track down. Remember, the way you format a program does not make any difference to the compiler. It uses certain rules for compiling the code. These rules are constant and are used all the time.

> **Note**
>
> The moral of the story is that the C programming language always associates an `else` with the closest preceding `if` statement.

In listing 5.6, the code is formatted to make it obvious as to what should occur (or at least partly obvious). Don't allow the code formatting to confuse you as to a statement's purpose. Incorrectly formatted code creates a logical error that can be difficult to track down.

> **Caution**
>
> Don't use too many if...else statements—nested if...else statements can be ambiguous. Too many of these will only confuse you and possibly introduce a logical error.

The *switch* Statement

You can make some decisions using the if or if...else statements. Sometimes, however, the resulting code can be difficult to follow and can confuse even an advanced programmer. The C programming language has a built-in, multiple-branch decision statement called switch. The switch statement causes a particular group of statements to be chosen from several available groups. The switch statement is similar to the if...else statement, but has increased flexibility and a clearer format.

The *switch* Statement

The switch statement is similar to the case statement in Pascal or the Select...Case statement in Microsoft QuickBASIC. BASICA and GW-BASIC don't have an equivalent statement.

The general form of the switch statement is as follows:

```
switch (expression)
{

    case constant1 :
        statement1;
        break;

    case constant2 :
        statement2;
        break;

    case constant3 :
        statement3;
        break;

        .

        .

        .

    case constantX :
        statementX;
        break;
```

```
          default :
              default statement;
     }
```

In the switch statement, the computer tests a variable consecutively against a list of integer or character constants. After finding a match, the computer executes the statement or block of statements that are associated with the specified constant.

The default statement is executed if the compiler does not find a match in the list of constants. The default statement is optional. If default is not present and all matches fail, no action takes place. When finding a match, the computer executes the statements associated with the specified case until it reaches the break statement or the end of the switch statement.

Following each of the case keywords is an integer or character constant. This constant ends with a colon (not a semicolon). There can be one or more statements following each case keyword. The statements are not required to be enclosed in braces. However, the entire body of the switch statement must be enclosed in braces.

Listing 5.7 shows you how to use the switch statement to process keyboard commands (like those in a menu program). The program displays a menu on-screen and prompts the user to enter a value. It then displays a status message. In a real menu program, you would use a function call to execute the appropriate command, thus accomplishing the request of the user.

Listing 5.7   Sample Program Using the *switch* Statement

```
/**********************************************
   MENU.C - Show use of the switch statement.
 **********************************************/

#include <stdio.h>

int main()
{
   char ch;

   printf(" ***Main Menu***\n");
   printf("1. Word Processor\n");
   printf("2. Spreadsheet\n");
   printf("3. Database\n");
   printf("\n");
   printf("Your Choice: ");

   ch = getchar();
```

(continues)

Listing 5.7   Continued

```
    switch (ch)
    {
       case '1' :
            printf("\nExecuting Word processor\n");
            break;

       case '2' :
            printf("\nExecuting Spreadsheet\n");
            break;

       case '3' :
            printf("\nExecuting Database\n");
            break;

       default :
            printf("\nInvalid menu selection\n");
    }

    return 0;
}
```

Notice the use of the break statement at the end of each case. If you do not use the break statement, program flow continues to the next case. When several conditions use the same piece of code, continuing to the next case is helpful. Sometimes, the capability of the case statements to run together when no break statement is present enables you to write more efficient programs by avoiding duplication of code. Most of the time, however, this is not what you want to happen.

Listing 5.8 demonstrates how to use more than one case statement with a set of instructions.

Listing 5.8   Another Program Using *switch* Statements

```
/**************************************************
   SWITCH.C - Sample program using switch statements.
 **************************************************/

#include <stdio.h>

int main()
{
   char ch;

   printf("Do you wish to continue "
            "program execution (Y/N) ? ");

   ch = getchar();

   switch (ch)
```

```
    {
        case 'y' :
        case 'Y' :
            printf("\nThe answer was YES\n");
            break;

        case 'n' :
        case 'N' :
            printf("\nThe answer was NO\n");
            break;

        default :
            printf("\nWrong answer.\n");
    }

    return 0;
}
```

This program shows a common case (no pun intended) in which you have to respond to a letter selection from the user (Y for yes or N for no), yet you don't want to force the user to type the letter in a specific case. The SWITCH.C program uses the same code to process the key, whether the user entered the value in upper- or lowercase.

As you progress in your study of the C language, you will learn other ways to convert letters and methods from uppercase to lowercase and vice versa. For now, the previous programs give good examples of the switch statement.

Nested *switch* statements

As with the if and if...else statements, the switch statement can be nested. When you nest the statement, the switch statement is part of the statement sequence of an *outer* switch (the first switch statement). Even if the case constant of the inner switch and the outer switch contain common values, no conflicts arise.

The Nested *switch* Statement
The general format of the nested switch statement is

```
switch (expression)
{
    case constant1 :
        switch (another expression)
        {
            case constant1 :
                statement1;
                break;
```

(continues)

(continued)

```
            case constant2 :
                statement2;
                break;

            default :
                default statement;
        }

    case constant2 :
        statement2;
        break;


    case constant3 :
        statement3;
        break;
            .
            .
            .
    case constantX :
        statementX;
        break;

    default :
        default statement;
}
```

This general form probably looks familiar, because it is simply a switch statement inside another switch statement. The expression used for each switch statement is usually different.

The switch statement is a powerful element of the C programming language—it is actually the core statement used in advanced graphical operating environments such as OS/2 and Microsoft Windows. Although programming for this environment is a topic of its own, the core of most every program written for OS/2 and Microsoft Windows has a switch statement, usually nested with other switch statements.

The switch statement responds to messages from the user. For example, if the user presses the mouse button, the switch statement receives a message. The program then responds to the message appropriately.

The *break* Statement

You have seen the use of the break statement to exit the switch statement. You will see it used in more detail in the programs in Chapter 6. The break statement transfers control from the switch statement to the first statement following the switch statement. It can be used also inside an if or if...else statement.

Summary

You have studied the three fundamental decision-making statements in the C programming language. The next chapter takes an equally important look at programs that loop.

> **Note**
>
> If you have typed the example programs in this chapter and feel comfortable with the material presented, continue your exploration of the C programming language. Otherwise, examine the example programs a little closer. Either way, take a break and pick up the book tomorrow—after a well-deserved rest.

The following points were covered in this chapter:

- The three decision-making statements in the C programming language are the if statement, the if...else statement, and the switch statement.

- The if statement is the fundamental decision-making statement in the C programming language. It enables your program to test an expression and execute a statement or group of statements depending on the outcome of the test.

- The if statement can be used to execute a block of statements by surrounding the block with braces.

- A program can nest if statements by including an if statement inside another if statement. This allows for expanded decision-making capabilities.

- The if...else statement is an expanded version of the if statement. It takes action whether the expression is true or false.

- The if...else statement can be nested just like the if statement. When doing so, you must be careful to match the right else with the right if statement.

■ The switch statement causes a particular group of statements to be chosen and executed from several available groups. It also can cause several cases to use the same code, resulting in a more efficient use of your program's resources.

■ Because of the flexibility of the C programming language, the switch statement can be nested similarly to if and if...else. When this occurs, the switch statement is part of the statement sequence of a switch statement.

■ The break statement transfers control from a switch statement to the first subsequent statement in the program.

Chapter 6

Programs that Loop

The last chapter focused on the decision-making statements available in the C programming language. Just as important as the decision-making statements are the *program-flow statements,* which you learn about in this chapter.

In C programs, instructions are usually executed in the order in which they appear in a listing, from the beginning. Each instruction is executed once and only once. Programs of this type are not flexible or practical, because they do not include logical control structures.

Many programs require that a group of instructions be executed repeatedly, until a logical condition has been satisfied. This condition is known as *looping.* Sometimes the number of repetitions required is not known in advance, other times it is. You can have a situation in which a loop continues until a logical condition becomes true. All these operations can be executed with different types of looping statements—available in the C programming language.

Looping statements are used to control program flow. One of the chief strengths of a computer is its capability to perform repeated tasks rapidly, accurately, and without complaint. You can instruct the computer to do the same thing over and over again, millions of times if necessary.

There are three major program loop statements in the C programming language: the `for` loop, the `while` loop, and the `do...while` loop. Each of them is discussed in turn. You will also learn the different varieties of each type of loop, as well as examine other statements used in the three main looping constructions.

The *for* Loop

The for loop is the fundamental looping statement in C. It is often used for situations in which you want to execute a task a specific number of times. The for loop is the statement you use for this job—it appears in almost every programming language available. However, C gives you more power and flexibility (which means more complexity) than most languages.

The *for* Loop

The general form of the for statement is

```
for (initialization; condition; increment)
    statement;
```

The parentheses following the for keyword contain the necessary elements for the for statement. The *initialization* keyword is used to initialize an index parameter that controls looping action. The *condition* represents a condition that must be satisfied in order for the loop to continue execution. Finally, *increment* is a value that determines how much the index variable is incremented.

The body of the for loop is located in the statement section. You can use braces to enclose multiple statements, or list a single statement (as shown).

```
int x;
for (x=0; x<10; x++)
    printf("This will be displayed 10 times\n");
```

Caution

A common error when writing for loops is to place a semicolon between the loop expressions and the body of the loop. Don't do it. The result does not create a complex C statement, and therefore will not compile.

Basic *for* Statements

To get you started, listing 6.1 gives an example of a simple for loop. The listing displays the numbers from 1 to 100 on-screen.

Listing 6.1   An Example *for* Loop Program

```
/*****************************************
   FORLOOP.C - Simple for loop example.
 *****************************************/

#include <stdio.h>
```

```
int main()
{
    int x;

    for (x=1; x<=100; x++)
        printf("Iteration: %d \n", x);

    return 0;
}
```

This program declares an integer index variable called x. The core functionality of the program lies in the `for` loop:

```
for (x=1; x<=100; x++)
```

The loop initially sets the variable x to 1. The second part of the `for` statement checks whether x is less than or equal to 100. If x passes this test, the program calls the `printf()` function, which displays the iteration number. After the number is displayed on-screen, the program increments the variable x by 1, using the increment operator (++). The statement could easily have appeared like this:

```
for (x=1; x<=100; x=x+1)
```

This looping process repeats until x is greater than 100, at which time the loop terminates and the program ends.

There is no law that says the loop is required to always run in a positive direction. You can create a program that counts down simply by changing the increment operator. For example, listing 6.2 is a modification of the earlier program. It counts down from 100 to 1 on-screen.

Listing 6.2   An Example *for* Loop that Counts Down from 100

```
/****************************************
   COUNTDN.C - Counts down from 100 to 1.
****************************************/

#include <stdio.h>

int main()
{
    int x;

    for (x=100; x>0; x--)
        printf("%d \n", x);

    return 0;
}
```

These two programs just begin to show the versatility of the `for` statement. Notice that the decrement (--) operator is used in this example. The control variable is initialized to 100; then the program determines whether the variable is greater than 0. If it is greater than 0, the body of the loop displays the value of x. For each test, if the variable x is greater than 0, the loop continues executing. Finally, when x becomes 0, the loop is terminated and the program ends.

C does not restrict you to incrementing or decrementing the value of the control variable by one. You can use any type of assignment operator. For example, the next program (TENCOUNT.C) in listing 6.3 prints the numbers from 0 to 100, counting by 10 (0, 10, 20, 30, and so on).

Listing 6.3   A Program to Count to 100 by 10

```
/************************************************
    TENCOUNT.C - Displays numbers from 0 to 100,
                 counting by 10.
   ************************************************/

#include <stdio.h>

int main()
{
   int x;

   for (x=0; x<=100; x=x+10)
      printf("The variable x is equal to %d \n", x);


   return 0;
}
```

Notice that a C program has complete control of incrementing the control variable. A control variable can be modified in the loop, but it is usually considered poor style. However, the compiler does enable you to do so. Also, remember that any test can be used inside the condition section of the `for` statement. For example, the statement

```
for (x=3; x==25; x++)
   printf("x=%d", x);
```

starts the loop by initializing the variable x to the value 3. The loop continues as long as x is equal to 25. For each time through the loop, x is incremented by one (with the increment operator). Unfortunately, this is a useless loop statement because the code following the `for` statement will never be executed. Your program never allows x to equal 25, therefore the `printf()` function in this code is never executed.

The moral of the story is that although you have great flexibility with for loops, you also have to be careful with the values you pass to the statement. If not, unexpected results can occur.

For example, if you have a statement such as

```
for (x=11; x<10, x++)
    printf("this will never be displayed\n");
```

the body of the loop will not be executed. The reason is because x starts at 11 and is incremented. At the same time, the code executes the body of the loop only when x is less than 10. Therefore nothing happens. These statements are a waste of memory—the body of the loop is never executed.

The ANSI C standard does not require any statement to follow the for statement. This means that the body of the for loop can be empty. You can use this fact to create time delays in your code. For example, this statement:

```
for (t=0; t< 999; t++)
    ;
```

causes the program to sit in a loop while the variable t counts from 0 to 999. No statements are executed, but the computer will be busy crunching numbers. As mentioned, this is a quick and dirty method for creating a time delay.

If you are working with real-time programming, be careful. The preceding loop will take different amounts of time to execute on different computers. An obvious example is if you compile the program on a PC, and then recompile the source code on a Cray supercomputer. Execution speeds will be drastically different, resulting in a different delay.

All the preceding examples have used a single statement in the body of the loop. It is possible for more than one statement to be used in the for loop by enclosing the block of statements in curly braces ({ and }). The following program (AVG.C) in listing 6.4 calculates the average of five, user-entered numbers.

Listing 6.4   A Loop to Calculate the Average of Five Numbers

```
/************************************************
   AVG.C - Averages five numbers entered by user.
 ************************************************/

#include <stdio.h>

int main()
{
    int counter;
```

(continues)

Listing 6.4   Continued

```
const int max = 5;
float x, average, sum = 0;

printf("This program will prompt you ");
printf("for five numbers\n");
printf("It will then display the ");
printf("average of these five numbers\n\n");

for (counter=1; counter<=max; counter++)
{
    printf("\nEnter number value of %d: ", counter);
    scanf("%f", &x);
    sum = sum + x;
}

average = sum / max;

printf("\nThe average of the "
        "numbers is %f", average);


    return 0;
}
```

The program in listing 6.4 uses the `for` statement to prompt the user to type five numbers. Each time through the loop, the program prompts the user to enter a value. The program then stores the value in x and adds the value to the running total stored in the variable sum. After the loop ends, the program divides the variable sum by the number of values entered (the integer constant max, equal to 5). Finally, the program displays the results to the user before the program terminates.

The important element of listing 6.4 is the use of braces around the three statements that form the body of the `for` loop:

```
for (counter=1; counter<=max; counter++)
{
    printf("\nEnter value of number %d : ", counter);
    scanf("%f", &x);
    sum = sum + x;
}
```

This group of statements, from beginning brace to ending brace, is treated as a single statement by the compiler. Notice that each statement in the block is a C statement and must be terminated with a semicolon. However, the entire block is not terminated with a semicolon.

The C programming language allows several variations that increase the power of `for` loops even more. One of the more common variations is the capability to use two or more control variables. The program (TWOVARS.C) in listing 6.5 shows how two variables are initialized at the same time in the initialization section of the for statement.

Listing 6.5   An Example of Initializing Several Variables in a *for* Loop

```
/***********************************************
   TWOVARS.C - Initializes several variables
               in the for loop.
 ***********************************************/

#include <stdio.h>

int main()
{
   int counter, total;

   for (counter=0, total=0; counter<=100;
     counter=counter + 10)
   {
     total = total + 1;
     printf("counter = %d and total = %d\n",
         counter, total);
   }

   return 0;
}
```

When the program in listing 6.5 is executed, the output looks something like this:

```
counter =   0 and total = 1
counter = 10 and total = 2
counter = 20 and total = 3
counter - 30 and total - 4
counter = 40 and total = 5
counter = 50 and total = 6
counter = 60 and total = 7
counter = 70 and total = 8
counter = 80 and total = 9
counter = 90 and total = 10
counter = 100 and total = 11
```

The variables counter and total are both initialized inside the for loop statement. Although the variable total was not used as an index variable in the loop, it can still be initialized at the beginning of the loop. This is one of the nice things about C—it does not force you to use any specific style. As mentioned before, C gives you lots of flexibility.

The output of the program displays the value of the counter, as well as the number of times the loop was executed.

Nested *for* Statements

Just as decision-making statements can be nested, so can program-flow statements. A nested for statement includes a for statement in another for statement. To demonstrate this structure, listing 6.6 presents a short program that displays a multiplication table.

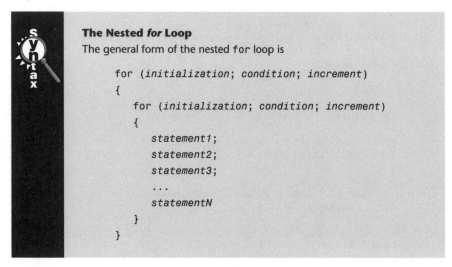

The Nested *for* Loop
The general form of the nested for loop is

```
for (initialization; condition; increment)
{
    for (initialization; condition; increment)
    {
        statement1;
        statement2;
        statement3;
        ...
        statementN
    }
}
```

Listing 6.6 contains an example of a nested for statement.

Listing 6.6   A Nested *for* Statement that Displays a Multiplication Table

```
/*********************************************
   MTABLE.C - Displays a multiplication table.
 *********************************************/

#include <stdio.h>

int main()
{
   int column, row;

   for (row=1; row<=10; row++)
   {
      for (column=1; column<=10; column++)
         printf(" %5d", column * row);
      printf("\n");
   }


   return 0;
}
```

The program displays a table that looks something like this:

```
 1   2   3   4   5   6   7   8   9  10
 2   4   6   8  10  12  14  16  18  20
 3   6   9  12  15  18  21  24  27  30
 4   8  12  16  20  24  28  32  36  40
 5  10  15  20  25  30  35  40  45  50
 6  12  18  24  30  36  42  48  54  60
 7  14  21  28  35  42  49  56  63  70
 8  16  24  32  40  48  56  64  72  80
 9  18  27  36  45  54  63  72  81  90
10  20  30  40  50  60  70  80  90 100
```

This multiplication table is suitable for teaching youngsters multiplication and is available for framing in a variety of sizes. The secret behind creating the table is in the nested `for` loop statements.

The numbers in the left column and top row serve as the labels of the multiplication table. If you go to the intersection point of a row and a column, you find the product of the two numbers. For example, start at 6 on the top column and go down seven rows to the intersection of 6 and 7. You find the number 42, because 6 multiplied by 7 is equal to 42.

Listing 6.6 creates two loops: an inner loop and an outer loop. The inner loop steps through 10 columns, from 1 to 10, whereas the outer loop steps through 10 rows. For each row, the inner loop executes once, then a carriage return is displayed to prepare for the next line of the table.

Each time through the inner loop—at the intersection of each column and row—the program multiplies the two numbers and displays the product in the table. To make sure the columns line up correctly, a field-width specifier of 5 is used in the `printf()` function.

> **Note**
>
> The rule for nested `if` statements applies equally well to nested `for` loops—a program block is associated with the closest preceding `for` statement.

You have examined several different variations of the `for` loop. Notice that each `for` loop requires that you always perform the conditional test at the beginning of the loop. This means that the program will never execute the code inside the loop if the condition tested is false. Next, you will study some program-flow structures that enable you to control when the test is executed.

The *while* Loop

The second type of loop available in the C programming language is the `while` loop.

The *while* Loop

The general form of the while statement is

```
while (expression)
    statement;
```

An example follows:

```
while (x == TRUE)
    printf("The variable x is TRUE");
```

The reserved word while is followed by an expression surrounded by parentheses. The statement can be a single statement followed by a semicolon or a block of statements surrounded by braces.

In the while loop, the body of the loop is executed as long as the expression is true. When the expression becomes false, program control passes to the line that follows the loop.

Listing 6.7 shows a program that produces similar results to listing 6.1 except it uses the while statement. It counts from 1 to 100, displaying the numbers on-screen.

Listing 6.7   A Sample Program Using the *while* Loop

```c
/***************************************************
   WHILE.C - Example of counting from 1 to 100.
***************************************************/

#include <stdio.h>

int main()
{

    int counter = 1;

    while (counter <= 100)
    {
        printf("Iteration: %d\n", counter);
        counter++;
    }

    return 0;
}
```

Listing 6.7 has many of the same elements of the simple program that demonstrated the for statement. Notice how you would initialize an index variable (counter) and increment it in the loop.

The program can be written more precisely, as follows:

```
#include <stdio.h>

int main()
{
   int counter = 1;

   while (counter <= 100)
      printf("Iteration: %d\n", counter++);

   return 0;
}
```

When executed, this program generates the same output as the first; however, it is several lines shorter. As is usual with the C programming language, you can produce the same results with fewer code instructions. Instead of incrementing the index value as a statement, the second example shows it as part of the printf() function call. By doing this, the programmer can use a single statement as the target of the while loop.

You can easily argue that either looping method—the for statement or the while statement—is easier to use. Each statement has its own place and time that it should be used. Many times these statements can be used interchangeably, as you have just seen.

Take a look at a different type of example. Listing 6.8 (TYPE0.C) loops until the user types the number 0.

Listing 6.8   A Program that Quits When the User Presses the Zero Key

```
/*********************************************
   TYPE0.C - Demonstrates the while loop.
*********************************************/

#include <stdio.h>

int main()
{
   int x = 1;

   while (x != 0)
   {
      printf("Enter a number, type 0 to quit\n");
      scanf("%d", &x);
   }

   return 0;
}
```

The TYPE0.C program does not know how many times the user will type a number other than 0. Therefore, the `while` loop continues to loop until a certain condition is met. As long as the user does not type 0, the loop continues to be executed.

The `while` loop differs from the `for` loop in that there is no initialization section for the `while` statement. The initialization must be done separately—as is shown in listing 6.8 when x is initialized to 1. It can be initialized to any variable other than 0 and the program will still work. The initialization is to make sure that the number is not 0, in which case the loop would never execute.

Listing 6.9 uses a `while` loop to check each character in a string. If the character is the null-terminating character, you exit the loop. You can then determine how long the string is.

Listing 6.9   Finding the Number of Characters in a String with the *while* Loop

```
/****************************************************
    COUNT.C - Counts number of characters in a string.
 ****************************************************/

#include <stdio.h>

int main()
{
    int count = 0;
    char str[255];

    printf("Type in a word :\n");
    scanf("%s", &str);

    while (str[count] != '\0')
        count++;

    printf("\nThe word was %d "
            "characters long\n", count);

    return 0;
}
```

Here is a sample interaction with the program:

```
Type in a word :
CisForMe

The word was 8 characters long
```

The program uses the `scanf()` function to query the user to type a string. It then counts how many characters are in the word. A `while` loop is used to start at the beginning of the string and count until a terminating null character is found (`\n`). The program then reports the number of characters in the word. Notice that the string must not be separated by spaces because the `scanf()` function would interpret the space as the beginning of a new string.

Nested *while* Loops

Just as `for` loops can be nested, so can `while` loops. By now you know what is meant by the term *nested*. Nested `while` loops enable you to put a `while` loop inside another `while` loop.

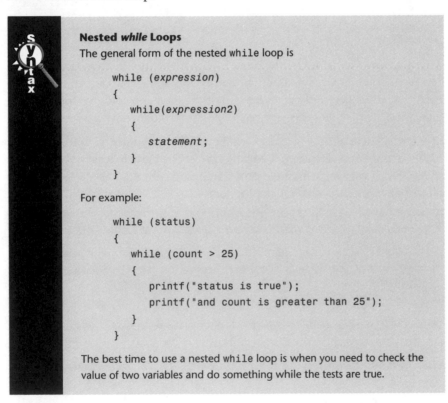

Nested *while* Loops

The general form of the nested while loop is

```
while (expression)
{
    while(expression2)
    {
        statement;
    }
}
```

For example:

```
while (status)
{
    while (count > 25)
    {
        printf("status is true");
        printf("and count is greater than 25");
    }
}
```

The best time to use a nested while loop is when you need to check the value of two variables and do something while the tests are true.

The *do...while* Loop

The last type of loop in C is the `do...while` loop. This loop structure is similar to the `while` loop. Unlike the `for` and `while` loops, which test the loop condition at the top of the loop, the `do...while` loop checks its condition at the end of the loop. This means that a `do...while` loop will always execute at least once.

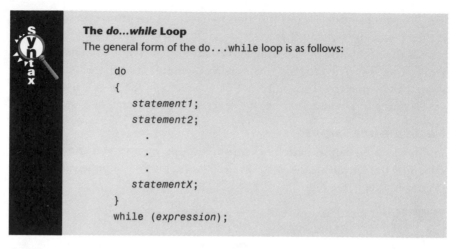

The *do...while* Loop

The general form of the do...while loop is as follows:

```
do
{
    statement1;
    statement2;
        .
        .
        .
    statementX;
}
while (expression);
```

The do...while loop, unlike the other loop statements you have examined, has two keywords: do and while. The do keyword marks the beginning of the loop. The while keyword marks the end of the loop and contains the loop expression. Notice that the do...while loop is terminated with a semicolon.

The statements enclosed in braces will be executed repeatedly, as long as the value of *expression* is true (not equal to zero). The curly braces ({ }) are required when working with a block of statements—the do...while loop is almost always used with a block of statements.

> **Note**
>
> Although braces are not necessary in the do...while loop when only one statement is present, they are frequently used to improve the overall readability of the statement.

Listing 6.10 is equivalent to listing 6.1, except it uses the do...while loop construction to display the numbers from 1 to 100.

Listing 6.10   Counting from 1 to 100 with the *do...while* Loop

```
/******************************************
    DOWHILE.C - Sample do...while loop.
******************************************/

#include <stdio.h>

int main()
{
    int x = 1;

    do
```

```
    {
       printf("%d\n", x++);
    }
    while ( x <= 100);

    return 0;
}
```

The important point to notice about this program is that the body of the loop will always be executed at least once because the test condition is at the end of the loop. If you are familiar with the Pascal programming language, you may think that the do...while loop is similar to the repeat...until statement. The difference is that the repeat...until statement loops *until* the test condition is true, whereas the do...while loop continues to loop *while* the test condition is true.

For most applications, it is more natural to test for continuation of the loop at the beginning rather than at the end of the loop. For this reason, the do...while statement is used less frequently than the other looping statements covered in this book.

Arrays and Loops

Looping structures are an ideal method for quickly accessing array elements. Because an array has an index value, a loop can be used to increment through each element of the array. Listing 6.11 shows an example.

Listing 6.11 Moving Through an Array with Loops

```
/**************************************************
   LOOPS.C - Example of using loops with arrays.
 **************************************************/

#include <stdio.h>
#include <limits.h>

int main()
{
   int numbs[10], count, avg;
   int total = 0, smallest = INT_MAX, largest = 0;

   /* introduction */
   printf("This is a program to average numbers.\n");
   printf(" You will be asked for 10\n");
   printf("numbers.\n\n");

   /* Get the 10 numbers */
   for (count=0; count<10; count++)
   {
      printf("Please enter number %d: ", (count+1) );
      scanf("%d", &numbs[count]);
      total = total + numbs[count];
   }
```

(continues)

Listing 6.11 Continued

```
/* Calculate average */
avg = total/10;

/* Find the largest and smallest numbers */
/*    by going through the entire array    */
/*    using a do...while loop.             */
count = 0;
do
{
   if (numbs[count] > largest)
        largest = numbs[count];

   if (numbs[count] < smallest)
        smallest = numbs[count];

   count++;
}
while (count<10);

/* display output to user */
printf("\n\nResults\n"
    "-------n");

printf("The average value is %d\n", avg);
printf("The numbers added equal %d\n", total);
printf("The largest number "
      "entered was %d\n", largest);
printf("The smallest number "
      "entered was %d\n", smallest);

return 0;

}
```

Here is a sample interaction with the program:

```
This is a program to average numbers.
You will be asked for 10
numbers.

Please enter number 1: 5
Please enter number 2: 10
Please enter number 3: 15
Please enter number 4: 5
Please enter number 5: 10
Please enter number 6: 15
Please enter number 7: 5
Please enter number 8: 10
Please enter number 9: 15
Please enter number 10: 10
```

```
Results
- - - - - - -
The average value is 10
The numbers added equal 100
The largest number entered was 15
The smallest number entered was 5
```

The program gets 10 numbers from the user and then displays information about those numbers to the user, including the average value, the sum of the numbers, the largest number entered, and the smallest number entered. The program uses a for loop to go through the array and prompt the user for the numbers.

The code to get the values from the user looks like this:

```
for (count=0; count<10; count++)
{
  printf("Please enter number %d: ", (count+1) );
  scanf("%d", &numbs[count]);
  total = total + numbs[count];
}
```

Notice that printf() adds 1 to the count variable. The reason for this is that arrays in C always start at index 0, yet it would be odd for a program to ask the user to "enter number 0." This is why the program adds 1 to the numeral displayed to the user.

The scanf() function reads the value into the current array element. A variable named total determines the total of the sum of all numbers entered. After the user enters all the numbers, the average value is calculated by subtracting the total sum from the total number of entries.

A do...while loop is then used to find the largest and smallest number. Another for loop could have been used, but it was a good opportunity to show the use of a different type of statement. Finally, the program uses a series of printf() statements to display the findings of the program.

Infinite Loops

Infinite loops are loops that continue on forever. The only way to stop a program that has an infinite loop is to abort the program in an unnatural way. Some compilers have a special option for break checking. When break checking is on, the compiler will check for the press of the Break key in the program and terminate the program if the Break key is pressed. If your compiler does not have break checking, the only way to end a program that has an infinite loop is to restart the computer.

Infinite loops are useful at times to force a program to continue running for an extended length of time. The infinite loop is a quick way to force the instructions to be repeated several times.

To create an infinite loop with the `for` statement, don't use any value for the three control variables. For example:

```
for (;;;)
    printf("this will continue to print forever\n");
```

To do the same thing with a `while` loop, use code like this:

```
while (1)
{
    printf("this will continue to print forever\n");
}
```

Finally, to accomplish an infinite loop in a `do...while` loop, write code that looks like this:

```
do
{
    printf("this will continue to print forever\n");
}
while (1);
```

Exiting an Infinite Loop

You could write your own code to exit out of an infinite loop, using C's `break` statement, first introduced in Chapter 5, "Programs that Make Decisions." Whenever the `break` statement is encountered anywhere inside the body of a loop, it causes immediate program termination. For example, you could re-write a `for` loop to look like this:

```
char ch;

for (;;;)
{
    printf("this will continue to print forever\n");
    printf("unless you press the letter 'A' now\n");
    scanf("%c", &ch);
    if (ch=='A')
        break;
}
```

This loop will continue to run until you type A in response to the message. If you press any other key, the program continues to loop.

Labels and the *goto* Statement

If you are familiar with programming with any language, you might be surprised to see the "dreaded" `goto` statement showing up in a language as prestigious as C. The use of the `goto` statement is looked on by many programmers as an inferior style of coding, because it leads to poorly structured programs.

However, the designers of the C programming language included the goto statement because, in their own words, "There are a few situations in which goto may find a place."

The problem with programs that use the goto statement is that the code is generally more difficult to understand and to update than code written without goto statements. That is why it is looked down on by many programmers.

The *goto* Statement

The goto statement is used to alter the normal sequence of program execution by transferring control to some other part of the program. In its general form, the goto statement is written as follows:

```
goto label;
```

whereby *label* is an identifier used to label the target statement that will receive the control. The target statement must be labeled, and the label must be followed by a colon. Each statement in the program must have a unique label. No two statements can have the same label. The target statement appears as:

```
label:
    statement;
```

For example:

```
int main()
{
label:
    printf("X");
goto label;
```

This example creates an infinite loop that repeatedly displays the letter *X* on-screen.

Caution

Make sure that each statement in your goto program has a unique label. No two statements can have the same label; if there are two statements with the same label, the compiler will issue an error message.

Listing 6.12 shows how to use the goto statement in a program.

Listing 6.12   An Example of the *goto* Statement

```
/*********************************************
  TRYGOTO.C - Example of the goto statement.
*********************************************/

#include <stdio.h>

int main()
{
    int counter = 0;

try_again:

    if (counter > 100)
        goto stop;

    printf("%d\n", counter);
    ++counter;
    goto try_again;

stop:

    return 0;
}
```

Listing 6.12 counts from 0 to 100. If you compare this program to listings 6.1 and 6.7, you will probably find that this program is not as easy to understand. Execution is not smooth because it jumps from location to location.

> **Note**
>
> Avoid using the goto statement—use instead an appropriate looping statement. In every case, you should be able to find a more elegant method using one of the looping structures. Because the goto statement creates unstructured programs, you will not see it used in any other place in this book.

The *break* Statement

The break statement has several uses. Its first purpose was to terminate a case statement, as you learned in Chapter 5, "Programs that Make Decisions." Its second purpose is to force immediate termination of a loop, therefore bypassing the normal loop conditional test.

When the compiler encounters the break statement inside a loop, the computer terminates the loop and program control resumes at the statement that follows the loop. Take a look at listing 6.13.

Listing 6.13   Using the *break* Statement in a Program

```
/*********************************************
   TRYBREAK.C - Example of the break statement.
*********************************************/

#include <stdio.h>

int main()
{
    int x;

    for (x=0; x<100; x++)
    {
       printf("variable x equals %d\n", x);
       if (x==10)
            break;          /* exit loop */
    }

    return 0;
}
```

The output of this program looks like this:

```
variable x equals 0
variable x equals 1
variable x equals 2
variable x equals 3
variable x equals 4
variable x equals 5
variable x equals 6
variable x equals 7
variable x equals 8
variable x equals 9
variable x equals 10
```

The program prints the value of the variable, from 0 to 10, then terminates.
This occurs because the break statement causes immediate exit from the loop.
The break statement overrides the conditional test x<100. It is important to
understand that a break statement will cause an exit from only the innermost
loop. For example:

```
for (x=0; x<50; ++x)
{
    count = 1;
    for(;;;)
    {
       printf("count is %d\n", count);
       count++;
       if (count==10)
          break;
    }
}
```

This will display the values of count 1 through 10 on-screen 100 times. Each time the computer encounters the break statement, the program passes control back to the outer for loop.

> **Note**
>
> The break statement exits from the innermost loop only. The next outer loop receives control after the break is done executing.

The *continue* Statement

The continue statement is used to bypass the remainder of a pass through a loop. It executes similarly to the break statement. However, instead of forcing termination, continue forces the next iteration of the loop to take place and skips any code in between.

The continue statement can be used with program-flow statements as well. The continue statement works similarly to the break statement. However, instead of forcing loop termination, the continue statement forces the next iteration of the loop to take place, and skips any code in between.

For example, take a look at listing 6.14.

Listing 6.14   An Example of the *continue* Statement

```
/***********************************************
   CONTIN.C - Example of continue statement.
***********************************************/

#include <stdio.h>

int main()
{
   int x;

   for (x=0; x<50; x++)
   {
      if (x%2)
         continue;
      printf("variable x equals %d\n", x);
   }

   return 0;
}
```

The output of this program looks like this:

```
variable x equals 0
variable x equals 2
variable x equals 4
```

```
variable x equals 6
variable x equals 8
variable x equals 10
variable x equals 12
variable x equals 14
variable x equals 16
variable x equals 18
variable x equals 20
variable x equals 22
variable x equals 24
variable x equals 26
variable x equals 28
variable x equals 30
variable x equals 32
variable x equals 34
variable x equals 36
variable x equals 38
variable x equals 40
variable x equals 42
variable x equals 44
variable x equals 46
variable x equals 48
```

Each time the program generates an odd number, the `if` statement executes because an odd number modulus 2 is always true. Therefore, an odd number causes the `continue` statement to execute, which causes the next iteration to occur, bypassing the `printf()` function and displaying only the even numbers.

The `continue` statement works a little differently in `while` and `do...while` loops. In this case, the `continue` statement causes program control to go directly to the conditional test and then continue the looping process. In the case of the `for` loop, the computer first performs the increment part of the loop. Then the computer performs the conditional test, all before the loop continues.

The `continue` statement can be used to quicken the termination of a loop by forcing the computer to perform a conditional test as soon as it encounters some terminating condition.

Summary

In this chapter, you focused on program-flow statements. You learned the commands used in the C programming language to direct the flow of a program. You also learned the three basic program control statements and how they are used. Specifically, the following important points were covered:

- There are three basic program control statements in the C programming language. They are the `for` loop, the `while` loop, and the `do...while` loop.

■ The `for` loop is the fundamental looping statement in C. It can have a single statement terminated by a semicolon or a block of statements surrounded by braces as its body. You can also nest the `for` statement. The `while` statement is used in a program in which you do not know how many times the loop will have to execute.

■ The `do...while` statement is similar to the `while` statement, except that its logical test is at the end of the loop. Therefore, the body of the loop is always executed at least once.

■ The `goto` statement is included in the C language because sometimes it is the only solution to a certain condition. However, the `goto` statement should not be relied on to change program flow. It results in the creation of unstructured programs.

■ The `continue` statement forces the next iteration of the loop to take place and skips any code in between.

■ Each of the three program control statements can be nested in themselves. When the statement is nested, it means that another loop is embedded in the outer loop.

Chapter 7

Modular Programming with Functions

Functions are the core of the C programming language. C is extensible and expandable because of functions. In this chapter, you examine the syntax, format, and purpose of functions. You learn about the standard library of functions included with every ANSI C compiler. Most important, you learn how to use functions to convert your programs to logical units that fit together like a puzzle.

The Concept of Functions

A *subprogram* is an important concept associated with a high-level programming language. Subprograms—or *functions,* as they are called in the C programming language—are the basis of all heavy-duty computer programming languages. Programmers who have used Pascal, FORTRAN, and modern versions of BASIC should already be familiar with functions.

Pascal uses functions and procedures. The C programming language does not have the concept of *procedures* (a subprogram that returns no value). All subprograms are called functions. However, you can inform your program that your function does not return a value. Therefore, C functions have the capabilities of *both* functions and procedures in Pascal.

A *structured program* consists of subprograms that create a working program when combined. Most programs written today are made up of subprograms. A function simply is a means of separating program logic into small parts.

The idea behind a function is separating each section of code that performs a specific task and treating that section as a separate entity. Then, whenever you have to accomplish the task that the function carries out, you simply call the function. A function can be called as many times as necessary.

A function is given its own name and accessed by that name. Data can be passed to a function, and the function then can operate on that data. In Chapter 2, "Your First Program," you were introduced to functions. The `main()` function definition of every program is considered to be a function to which the operating system passes control when a program starts running.

You have already used the built-in *library functions,* but you might not have guessed that they were functions. These general-purpose functions come with the compiler. Examples of library functions are `printf()`, `scanf()`, `gets()`, and `puts()`. A great many functions are included with the standard definition of the C language; these library functions are not considered to be part of the C programming language.

The ANSI C definition provides a summary of *standard functions*—functions that should be included as standard on all ANSI-compatible C compilers. This way, you are assured that all C compilers have a base set of functions that act in the same manner and style.

Most C compilers add a large number of functions on top of those standard functions. These extended functions support the basic features of the computer on which they are running. For example, both Borland and Microsoft C compilers (which are available only on PC-based systems) include their own graphics libraries. These graphics libraries provide access to the graphics capabilities that are inherent to the PC system. Other compilers on different computers probably use different functions for their graphics routines.

> **Note**
>
> The unfortunate aspect of these libraries is that there is no standardization among manufacturers on the function names for these extended libraries. Therefore, a program that uses extended graphics functions on one compiler cannot be ported to a different system and recompiled quickly.

Using the Standard Library

The standard C function library provides routines for the most common programming tasks. The standard library functions provide a convenient interface to the language and a base level of functionality.

The function library is divided into smaller, related groups. For example, the time library includes functions for working with the date and time, and the standard I/O library includes functions that control computer input and output.

To use the functions in your own programs, all you have to do is include the appropriate header file at the beginning of your program. The header file contains the declarations of the functions. You execute the standard library functions by declaring their names, which you can do by including the appropriate header file at the beginning of the program. For example,

```
#include <math.h>
```

enables you to use the mathematical functions. The MATH.H file is inserted into your program and includes declaration for the available math functions.

Note

Remember that the #include statement is a preprocessor directive that tells the compiler to merge the specified header file into your source file during compilation. The included file is referenced when your program is being compiled.

The angle brackets surrounding the header file name tell the compiler to look in the standard library directory. In the preceding example, the file included is the MATH.H header file, which is used for standard input and output. You already have used library functions for many tasks in your programs up to this point, so using the function library should not be an entirely new concept.

The definitions for the standard library are divided among 15 header files. Each header file is responsible for a specific group of functions. Table 7.1 lists the header files and the types of functions that they declare.

Table 7.1 Header Files Included in the Standard C Library

Header File	Description
ASSERT.H	Allows diagnostics to be added to programs
CTYPE.H	Declares functions for testing characters
ERRNO.H	Defines constants for error conditions
FLOAT.H	Defines constants for floating-point arithmetic
LIMITS.H	Defines constants for sizes of data types
LOCALE.H	Includes functions that provide country and language information
MATH.H	Defines mathematical functions

(continues)

Table 7.1 Continued	
Header File	**Description**
SETJMP.H	Provides a way to change program flow with functions
SIGNAL.H	Includes functions for handling exception conditions
STDARG.H	Provides facilities for variable argument lists
STDDEF.H	Defines common data types and macros
STDIO.H	Provides facilities for standard input and output
STDLIB.H	Defines utility functions
STRING.H	Includes functions for working with character arrays
TIME.H	Includes date and time functions

Although the C standard library definitions are split among 15 header files, they can be divided into 10 main categories, as follows:

- *Input and output.* These functions handle the tasks of moving data into and out of your programs.

- *String and character.* These functions manipulate characters and character arrays (strings).

- *Mathematical.* These functions perform many of the common mathematical calculations that you might need.

- *Time and date.* These functions handle time and date functions as related to the operating system.

- *General utilities.* This is a group of basic C programming utility functions.

- *Character-handling.* These functions test character variables.

- *Diagnostics.* These functions enable you to troubleshoot bugs in your programs.

- *Nonlocal jumps.* These functions provide ways to avoid normal function call and return sequences.

- *Signal-handling.* These functions handle *exception conditions,* such as an interrupt signal or an error condition.

- *Variable-length argument lists.* These functions enable an unknown number of variables to be passed to a function.

The following sections describe each group of functions and explore how they are used.

Input and Output Functions

The input and output (I/O) functions represent almost one-third of the entire standard C library. The input and output functions declared in STDIO.H provide functions for the standard I/O devices (listed in table 7.2) and file I/O. The STDIO.H header file also declares file input and output. Both sequential and random-access file I/O is provided for, as you learn in Chapter 11, "Working with Files."

Table 7.2   Standard Streams Declared in STDIO.H

Stream Name	Description	Device
stdin	Input stream	Keyboard
stdout	Output stream	Video display
stdprn	Printer stream	Printer port
stdaux	Auxiliary output	Serial port
stderr	Error stream	Video display

String and Character Functions

The STRING.H header file declares functions that manipulate character arrays. Unlike other programming languages, which have a predefined string variable type (like BASIC), C does not have any explicit string type. Instead, all programs that use a group of characters also use character arrays (as you already know).

Because C does not have a string type, you cannot assign the value of one string to another. For example, the following code is invalid:

```
char a[99];
char b[99] = "Cannot do this";

a = b;  /* illegal operation */
```

Instead, a program has to use functions that copy the contents of one string to another string. Instead of using the preceding assignment statement, a C program uses code that looks something like this:

```
#include <string.h>

char a[99];
char b[99] = "This can be done";

strcpy(a, b);      /* Copy contents of variable b to variable a */
```

The STRING.H header file contains functions that are useful for comparing strings, finding the length of strings, and manipulating strings. Table 7.3 lists some of the most important string-manipulation functions available in the standard C string library.

Table 7.3	String-Manipulation Functions
Function	**Description**
strcmp()	Compares two strings
strlen()	Returns the length of a string
strcat()	Appends one string to another
strcpy()	Copies one string to another

Mathematical Functions

The header file MATH.H declares mathematical functions. These functions provide functionality beyond basic addition, subtraction, multiplication, and subtraction.

This file defines trigonometric functions, functions that find the square root of a number, and functions that find the logarithm of a number. The file also contains several miscellaneous functions for mathematical operations. Table 7.4 lists the most common functions.

Table 7.4	Mathematical Functions
Function	**Description**
abs()	Absolute value of an integer variable
fabs()	Absolute value of a floating-point number
sin()	Sine of a number
cos()	Cosine of a number
tan()	Tangent of a number
asin()	Arc sin of a number
acos()	Arc cosine of a number
atan()	Arc tangent of a number
log()	Natural logarithm

Function	Description
log10()	Base-10 logarithm
exp()	Exponential function
sqrt()	Square-root function
pow()	The power of a number

Although the mathematical functions provide a good base level of math capability, you might need more powerful math functions for specialized scientific or statistical programs. In this case, you have the choice of writing your own functions or purchasing third-party math libraries. These libraries are available with a number of different capabilities and at varying costs. Evaluate several of them before making a firm decision about which one to use.

Time and Date Functions

The TIME.H header file declares types and functions for manipulating the date and time. The main functions declared in the header file enable you to get the current system date and time from the operating system. The functions support several different time formats. The file also contains functions that convert time formats.

On UNIX-based machines, the date and time are expressed by the number of seconds elapsed since 00:00:00 hours Greenwich Mean Time (GMT) on January 1, 1970. This is a universal representation of the time. Table 7.5 lists some important time and date functions.

Table 7.5 Time and Date Routines	
Function	**Description**
stime()	Sets the system's time and date
time()	Gets the time in Greenwich Mean Time (GMT)
asctime()	Converts time from one data type to another
clock()	Returns elapsed processor time in clicks

General Utility Functions

The STDLIB.H header file provides functions that every C program will use. These functions include common data types, number conversion, and memory-storage allocation. Table 7.6 lists some of the most common functions declared in the STDLIB.H header file.

Table 7.6 General Utility Functions Declared in STDLIB.H	
Function	**Description**
rand()	Returns a random number
srand()	Returns a random number from a seed
exit()	Causes program to terminate
abort()	Causes program to terminate abnormally
malloc()	Allocates memory
realloc()	Reallocates memory
free()	Returns allocated memory to the system
system()	Executes an operating-system function
qsort()	Sorts an array, using the QuickSort algorithm

Character-Handling Functions

The CTYPE.H header file declares functions for testing characters, which are useful for determining what type of value is stored inside a char (character) variable. For example, the isupper() function returns a true value if the specified character is uppercase. The isdigit() function returns true if the number is a decimal digit. Table 7.7 lists some of the most useful character-handling functions.

Table 7.7 Character-Handling Functions	
Function	**Description**
isalpha()	Determines whether a character is alphabetic
iscntrl()	Determines whether a value is a control character
islower()	Determines whether a character is lowercase
ispunct()	Determines whether a value is a punctuation character
isspace()	Determines whether a value is a space character
isupper()	Determines whether a character is uppercase
islower()	Determines whether a character is lowercase
tolower()	Converts a character to lowercase
toupper()	Converts a character to uppercase

Diagnostics Functions

Although most compilers provide debugging tools, such as stand-alone debuggers, the C language defines functionality in the ASSERT.H header file for adding diagnostics services to a program. The only function declared is named (appropriately enough) `assert()`.

The *assert( )* Function

The format of `assert()` is as follows:

```
#include <assert.h>

assert(expression)
```

If *expression* fails (returns a false value), an error message is displayed on the standard error device, which usually is defined to be the screen.

Following is a specific example:

```
#include <assert.h>

int x;

printf("Enter a number greater than 5");
scanf("%d", &x);

assert(x>5)
```

If the number that the user enters is not greater than 5, a message is displayed on-screen in the following format:

```
Assertion failed: expression, file (filename),
line (linenumber)
```

The program is immediately aborted. The compiler supplies the *filename* and *linenumber,* whereas the *expression* is copied from the actual line of code. There is no way to change the message, other than the *expression, filename,* and *linenumber.*

Although there are more user-friendly ways to ensure that the value entered by the user is valid, when you are testing variables that are dependent on hardware, the `assert()` function is a handy method of checking for error values.

Nonlocal Jump Functions

Only a few functions are declared in the SETJMP.H header file. The `setjmp()` function provides a way to avoid a normal function call and return sequence.

Usually, this function is used to permit an immediate return from a deeply nested function.

Signal-Handling Functions

Many programs are written to handle system interrupts. In the SIGNAL.H header file, the C programming language provides facilities for processing these interrupts. Functions like these give C its power. Most high-level languages don't provide any way to handle system interrupts.

When you declare a signal handler, you use the `signal()` function. You provide the type of interrupt that you want `signal()` to handle, as well as the name of the function that you want `signal()` to call. The ANSI definition declares three types of interrupts that you can set. Table 7.8 lists the types of signals you can set and what those interrupts do.

Table 7.8 Types of Signal Handlers that a C Program Can Set	
Value	**Description**
SIG_DFL	Terminates the program
SIG_ERR	Indicates error return from signal
SIG_IGN	Ignores this signal type

Variable-Length Argument List Functions

Variable-length argument lists allow several values to be passed to a function. Whereas some functions, such as `puts()`, can take only one parameter, others can take any number of parameters. For example, `printf()` can take several parameters, depending on the contents of its first string, as shown in the following examples:

```
printf("number is %d", i);
                        /* two parameters */
printf("name is %s, number is %d", str, i);
                        /* three parameters */
```

The C programming language enables you to write functions that take a different number of arguments. Variable-length argument lists are unique to C. To declare variable-length argument lists, you must include the STDARG.H header file.

Now that you have learned the standard functions included with most C compilers, you are ready to learn how to write your own functions. This way, you can unleash the power of C, because all the functions you write are considered to be equal to the standard library functions. Therefore, when you write functions, you actually are extending the language, developing features and functions that the developers of C never thought of or needed.

A Simple Function

As defined earlier in this chapter, a function is a self-contained program in another program that carries out a specific, well-defined task. A program can contain multiple functions, each of which is considered to be a separate program.

Several reasons for using functions are that they help with the overall organization of a program, they reduce the memory overhead required by the compiler, and they enable you to create reusable code. Program organization is improved by dividing tasks into logical, well-defined functions. Functions help the programmer who is working as part of a team as well as the programmer who is working alone on a project.

The second important aspect of functions is their capability to reduce the memory required in a program. By calling a function instead of repeating the code every time a task has to be executed, a program uses less memory. Although computers now can be expanded to 16M (megabytes) of memory and beyond, creating memory-efficient programs still is a priority for most developers.

Finally, functions enable you to reuse code. Reusing code can save you many hours of programming time. Reuse refers to the practice of separating a program into well-defined tasks that compose the functions. Then you can use these functions for more than one programming project.

For example, almost every program that uses disk files must contain a section of code that asks the user for a file name and determines whether the file is present on the disk. By putting this task in a function, you eliminate a piece of code that you must write for your next program. As a result, programmers tend to build up large libraries of their favorite routines, which they can use to create new applications quickly.

Declaring the Function

The function carries out its intended action whenever it is accessed (or whenever the function is called from another portion of the program). The same function can be accessed from several different places in a program. After the function carries out its intended action, control returns to the point at which the function was accessed.

Note

A function usually contains three parts: the *function declaration,* the actual *function,* and the *function call.*

Function Declarations

Just as you can't use a variable without first informing the compiler what that variable is, you can't use a function without informing the compiler. The function usually is declared at the beginning of the program. The program declaration takes the following general format:

```
type function_name(type varname1,
                   type varname2,
                   ...,
                   type varnameX);
```

The declaration informs the compiler that at some point in the program, you plan to create a function with the name *function_name.* The first type keyword informs the compiler what data type the function returns. You can specify any C data type. If the function is not to return any value, use the keyword void.

The list of types and variable names in parameters are the arguments that are passed to the function. A function can be used without parameters, in which case the parameter list will be empty; the parentheses still are required, however. The function declaration ends with a semicolon. Following is a code example of a function declaration:

```
function void foo(int x);  /* declaration */
void foo(int x)
{
   printf("The value is %d" x);
}

int main()
{
   foo(3);
   return 0;
}
```

Unlike a variable declaration, in which many variables of a common type can be declared at the same time, such as

```
int dollars, cents, total;
```

all function parameters must include both the type and variable name. Following is the correct parameter declaration for the preceding variables when they are used as arguments in a function:

```
int dollars, int cents, int total
```

The Function Body

The second step in using a function is writing the body. Following is the general format:

```
type function_name(type varname1,
                   type varname2,
                   ..., type varnameX)
{
  /* body of function */
}
```

The first line of the function is virtually a copy of the function declaration, except that it is not followed by a semicolon. Again, all parameters must include both the type and variable name. The statements that form the body of the function are enclosed in braces.

> ### Note
>
> Don't make the common mistake of placing a semicolon after your function declaration. Doing so will introduce a bug into your program.

Calling the Function

When the function is written, you can use it in your program. Following is an example of the way a function is used in a program:

```
void main()
{
  /* other statements */

  function_name(var1, var2, ..., varX);

  /* more statements */

}
```

If you want to use the value returned by a function, put the function on the right side of an assignment statement, as follows:

```
value = function_name(var1, var2, ..., varX);
```

Listing 7.1 shows a program that uses a simple function.

Listing 7.1   A Program that Uses a Basic Function

```
/*****************************************************
    SIMPFUNC.C - A simple function used in a program.
    *
 *****************************************************/

#include <stdio.h>

void showdashes(void);    /* function declaration */

int main()
{
   printf("This is to be underlined\n");
   showdashes();      /* function call */
   printf("Hey, do that once again\n");
   showdashes();      /* function call */
   return 0;
}

/**********************/
void showdashes()
{
   printf("-----------------------\n");
}
```

When the program is executed, it displays four lines of output, as follows:

This is to be underlined

Hey, do that once again

Notice that the function was called twice, thereby saving the hassle of typing the code twice as well as the memory required to store it twice.

The preceding function, named showdashes(), is the simplest type of function that a C program can use. The function doesn't return a value and is not passed any values from the main program. Although a simple function may help you organize a program, functions are useless unless you can receive values from them and pass values to them.

Functions that Return a Value

Some functions, such as showdashes(), don't return any data, whereas other functions can return values. The return statement is used to return a value from a function.

The return function actually has two uses. First, return causes an immediate exit from the current function—that is, program flow returns to the statement after the function call. Second, return is used to return a value to the program.

Program execution in a function usually ends when the compiler finds the closing brace in the function. You can force a function to return to the calling program at a specific point by using the return statement.

To return a value from a function, you must follow the return statement with the value to be returned. The following function returns the absolute value (removes the negative sign) of a number.

```c
int absolute(int number)
{
  int result;
  if (number>1) return number;
      /* If number is positive, return now. */

  result = -number;
      /* Make number positive. */

  return result;
}
```

Listing 7.2 is a full-blown example of using the function in a program.

Listing 7.2   A Program To Return a Value from a Function

```c
/****************************************************
   RETVAL.C - Example program that returns a
              value from a function.

   ***************************************************/

#include <stdio.h>

int absolute(int number);  /* Function declaration */

int main()
{
   printf("%d\n", absolute(9) );   /* Test function */
   printf("%d\n", absolute(-9) );
   printf("%d\n", absolute(0) );

   return 0;
}


/***************************************/
int absolute(int number)  /* Body of function */
```

Listing 7.2   Continued

```
{
   int result;
   if (number>0)        /* Is number positive? */
      return number;    /* If so, return now */

   result = number - number - number;
                        /* Make it positive */

   return result;
         /* Return value to calling function. */

}
```

The main() section of the program feeds a couple of numbers into the function to make sure that the function works. The output of the program is as follows:

```
9
9
0
```

If your output does not come out this way, check the program to make sure that you entered everything correctly.

Each time the function is called, it is passed an integer value. Inside the function, this value is referred to as the variable number. Because functions are considered to be separate program modules, however, you could have a variable with the same name in main(), and the compiler would access it as though it were a variable with a different name.

Inside the function, a test is made to determine whether the value passed to the function is positive. If the value is positive, the function does not have to do anything; it returns to the calling program immediately, using the return statement. The calculation makes the number positive by calculating the inverse of the number (-number).

The result of the calculation then is returned to the main program with the return statement, followed by the value to be passed back (in this case, the variable result).

Passing Data to a Function

The information to be passed to a function is called an *argument* (also called a parameter). Now that you have returned data from a function, you are ready to learn how to pass data to a function. The last program gave you a sneak preview of this procedure. After you declare the data types of the arguments in the program, you can access them with the specified variable name. Listing 7.3 (PASSDAT.C) shows a function that is passed two numbers and that returns the sum of the numbers.

Listing 7.3   A Function To Add Two Numbers

```c
/****************************************************
   PASSDAT.C - Pass data to a function with arguments.

   ****************************************************/

#include <stdio.h>

/* Function declaration */
int add(int num1, int num2);

int main()
{
   int result;
   result = add(1, 2);
   printf("1 + 2 is %d", result);

   return 0;
}


/*****************************/
int add(int num1, int num2)
{
   int result;  /* Local variable  */

   result = num1 + num2;
                /* Actual calculation  */

   return result;

}
```

Although this function uses integer parameters, you could rewrite the function to use any of the regular data types. Following is the output of the program:

```
1 + 2 is 3
```

The program shows how multiple variables are used in the function. Notice that the variable declared as result is called a *local variable*, meaning that the variable is used only in the function. If you tried to access the variable in main(), the compiler would report an error. Later in this chapter, you learn methods of sharing variables throughout functions and programs.

Passing Arrays to a Function

You have learned how to pass standard data types to a function. This section shows how to pass arrays to your functions.

Passing Arrays

The program shown in listing 7.4 uses a bubble sort to sort an array of numbers. This program is an example of passing an integer array to a function.

Listing 7.4   A Bubble-Sort Routine

```
/*****************************************
   SORT.C - Sort an integer array.

 *****************************************/

#include <stdio.h>

void sort(int list[]);  /* function declaration */

const int MAX = 10;

int main()
{
   int count = 0, list[10];

   printf("You will be prompted for 10 numbers.\n");

   do
   {
      printf("Enter number %d: ", count+1);
      scanf("%d", &list[count++]);
   }
   while (count < MAX);

   sort(list);

   printf("\n\nResults\n");

   for (count=0; count<MAX; count++)
      printf("Position %d is now %d\n",
               count, list[count]);

   return 0;
}

/********************************/
void sort(int list[])
{
   int i, j, temp;
   for (i=0; i<MAX-1; i++)
   {
      for (j=i+1; j<MAX; j++)
      {
      if (list[i] > list[j])
      }
         temp = list[j];
         list [j] = list[i];
         list [i] = temp;
      }
```

```
            }
        }
    }
```

The output of the program looks similar to this:

```
You will be prompted for 10 numbers.
Enter number 1: 4
Enter number 2: 7
Enter number 3: 4
Enter number 4: 2
Enter number 5: 687
Enter number 6: 322
Enter number 7: 1
Enter number 8: 67
Enter number 9: 9
Enter number 10: 23


Results
Position 0 is now 1
Position 1 is now 2
Position 2 is now 4
Position 3 is now 4
Position 4 is now 7
Position 5 is now 9
Position 6 is now 23
Position 7 is now 67
Position 8 is now 322
Position 9 is now 687
```

The sorting algorithm is based on a bubble sort, whereby the lower numbers move slowly to the top of the list. The bubble sort is inefficient but simple to implement. The function, named sort(), is passed an array of numbers. This function then sorts the list.

This program may seem strange after the earlier discussion of returning values. A function can return only a standard data type; you cannot return an array directly. This program simply takes the array as an argument and then rearranges the array.

Nothing is returned because the actual addresses of the array are passed to the function. Passing the array to the function does not create a new copy of the array. Unlike local variables, which are separate between functions, the array is one and the same. When you modify the array in the function, you actually are modifying the original array.

The designers of C decided that it was a good idea to pass arrays this way, because creating an entirely new array would use a large portion of memory, as well as consume a great deal of processor time.

Visibility and Lifetime of Variables

Any variable declared inside a function can be used only by statements inside the function. If you declare a variable outside the functions, all the functions in the program can access that variable. Variables that can be accessed by all functions are called *global variables*.

Listing 7.5 shows a program that uses both *local variables* (variables inside a function) and *global variables* (functions declared for all functions in a program).

Listing 7.5   A Program To Show Some Uses of Global and Local Variables

```
/***************************************************
   GLOBAL.C - Demonstration of global and
              local variables.

   **************************************************/

#include <stdio.h>

void functioncall(void);   /* function declaration */

int number;                /* global variable */

int main()
{
   printf("starting main()\n");
   number = 10;
   printf("number is %d\n", number);
   functioncall();
   printf("number is %d\n", number);
   return 0;
}

/************************/
void functioncall()
{
   number = 25;
   printf("returning from function\n");
}
```

The output of the program looks like this:

```
starting main()
number is 10
returning from function
number is 25
```

This example creates a global variable, named number. This variable first is assigned the value 10 in main(); a function then assigns 25 to the variable. The value of the variable is displayed several times during execution of the program so that you can see how the variable changes.

Caution

You should take certain precautions when declaring and using global variables. Try to avoid making all your program's variables global. Otherwise, you will start creating functions that rely on certain global variables, and the functions cannot be used with other programs.

Although global variables can be handy, stay away from defining and using global variables unless absolutely necessary, because they cannot be used with other programs. Worse yet, if you have a global variable that is inadvertently modified by one function, other functions may react illogically, because the other functions expected the global variable to have a certain value. This bug is difficult to detect.

The *main( )* Function

You have seen the `main()` function declared many times by now. The function looks like this:

```
int main()
```

This declaration says that the function returns an integer value. The operating system uses this value to return an error condition. A zero value returned to the operating system means that no errors occurred.

You can specify other parameters to be passed from the operating system to the `main()` function when your program is called. These parameters are called *command-line arguments*. Command-line arguments are parameters that follow the program's name in the command line. For example, you usually can start an editor and specify the file to be edited at the same time. Use the following line, entered at an operating-system command-line prompt:

```
EDIT filename
```

`filename` is the name of the file that you want to edit. Many other programs enable you to do this trick. The operating system automatically passes any command-line parameters to the program being loaded.

Command-line arguments usually are used to pass information to a program when it runs. These parameters are passed to a program as parameters of the `main()` function.

This is the *only* time you use parentheses after the `main()` function (haven't you wondered what those parentheses were used for?). Following is the general format for accessing command-line arguments:

```
void main(int argc, char *argv[])
 {
 .
 .  /* variables are used in body of program  */
 .
 }
```

Two built-in arguments are used to receive command-line arguments. These arguments, argv[] and argc, are the only arguments that main() can have.

The argc parameter (short for *ARGument Count*) is an integer that holds the number of arguments passed on the command line. The argv[] parameter (short for *ARGument Values*) is a pointer to an array of character pointers. You have not yet learned pointers. All you have to know about them at this point, however, is that each element in the argv[] array corresponds to a command-line argument.

Listing 7.6 displays the number of command-line parameters passed to the program, as well as each command-line parameter.

Listing 7.6 A Program To Display Command-Line Arguments

```
/****************************************************
   COMLINE.C - Access command-line arguments.
      *
   ****************************************************/

#include <stdio.h>

int main(int argc, char *argv[])
{
   int counter;

   printf("Number of arguments: %d\n", argc);

   for (counter=0; counter<argc; counter++)
     printf("Argument %d is %s\n",
         counter, *(argv+counter) );

   return 0;
}
```

If you invoke this program by typing

```
COMLINE this is a test
```

the program should output something like this:

```
Number of arguments: 5
Argument 0 is C:\COMLINE.EXE
Argument 1 is this
Argument 2 is is
Argument 3 is a
Argument 4 is test
```

By convention, the first array element of argv[] always is the full path name of the program being executed. As a result, argc is the number of command-line arguments, plus one.

Being able to pass command-line arguments to a program is helpful to the user, because he or she can start the program and specify a file name at the same time. As you can see, it is not difficult to add this functionality to your program.

Summary

This chapter discussed how to use functions. You learned the syntax, the format, and the purpose of functions. You also learned about the standard library that comes with C compilers. In particular, this chapter covered the following important points:

- A *function* is a subprogram, or a program inside a program. Each function has its own variables, separate from the rest of the program.

- Functions are used to divide a program into logical units.

- Several reasons to use functions include the improved organization of a program, the reduction in memory size, and the capability to reuse program code.

- Library functions are general-purpose functions that accompany the compiler. The ANSI C language definition provides for certain libraries, which all compilers should support, as a base. These libraries are called the *standard libraries*.

- You can pass data into and out of functions. You also can pass arrays among functions.

- The return statement is used to pass a single value from the function to the line that called the function.

- The variables passed to a function are called *arguments* or *parameters*. These variables provide a means to pass information to the function.

- *Global variables* are variables that are declared outside any function and that can be accessed by all functions in a program.

- *Command-line arguments* are characters that appear after a program name at an operating-system command prompt. To access these arguments from a C program, use the argc (for argument count) and argv[] (argument values) parameters from the main() function.

■ The first command-line argument returned as `argv[0]` always is the full path name of the program. Multiple arguments are separated in the command line by spaces. To include characters separated by spaces, enclose the string in quotation marks.

Chapter 8

Preprocessor Directives

You can include various instructions for the C compiler in the source code of your program. These instructions, processed before the code is compiled, are called *preprocessor directives.* Preprocessor directives expand the scope of C beyond its basic definition. All preprocessor directives begin with the pound character (#).

The preprocessor directives are interpreted before the compilation process begins. Preprocessor directives usually appear at the beginning of a program and are grouped with other directives (although this is not required). The directives apply to the portion of the program following their appearance.

You have seen the line

```
#include <stdio.h>
```

in most of the programs in this book. This line instructs the compiler to include information about the standard input/output library. If you look at the STDIO.H file, you see that it looks like program code that would appear in your own program. This line appears at the beginning of most C source-code files.

The #include directive is only one of many available preprocessor directives. Others provide for macro definitions, conditional compilation, error generation, and line control. This chapter presents these preprocessor directives and examines how you can use them in your own programs.

File Inclusion

As you have seen, file inclusion is one of the most common preprocessor directives used in the C programming language. When a file is *included,* the contents of the include file are inserted at the current location of the source file.

The *#include* Directive

Following is the general format of file inclusion:

```
#include <filename.h>
```

The #include directive instructs the compiler to include another source file in the one that has the directive. The source file to be included is enclosed in angle brackets.

Another form of file inclusion uses the following format:

```
#include "filename.h"
```

This format, in which quotation marks are used around the file name, instructs the compiler to search the current directory for the file to be included. You must include the full path name and the extension of the file. The following example illustrates #include:

```
#include <stdio.h>
int main()
{
    printf("this function is in stdio.h");
    return 0;
}
```

Note

In C, the file to be included in your code (in this case, STDIO.H) is called a *header file,* or *header* for short. This naming convention reflects the fact that these declarations usually appear at the beginning of a program.

The angle brackets cause the preprocessor to search the default include file directory. The location of this directory is a default of the compiler and depends on what type of system and what C compiler you are using.

Note

The first style of file inclusion (with angle brackets) is used for standard header files. These header files are declared for the standard C library. The second style of file inclusion (with quotation marks) normally is used for header files that are specific to a program.

Header files usually are reserved for function prototypes, variable declarations, and other preprocessor directives. They rarely contain source code. The most common use of header files is for *function prototypes* (described in more detail in Chapter 7, "Modular Programming with Functions").

Macro Definitions

If file inclusion is the most common C preprocessor directive that you will encounter, macro definitions probably are the second most common type. Macro definitions usually are associated with word processing and spreadsheet programs. Macros save you time in carrying out your tasks. The C programming language includes its own macro facility.

Macros are part of the C preprocessor—that is, they are processed before the C compiler compiles the code. When the preprocessor encounters a macro, the macro name is replaced by a piece of code that performs an action. Macros can be used with or without arguments. Macros work similarly to functions, but they are not as versatile.

The #*define* Directive

When the preprocessor encounters a macro name, it replaces the macro name with another string that was previously defined. Use the following general format to define a macro:

```
#define identifier replacement_string
```

You have already seen the #define statement used to define symbolic constants in a C program. The #define statement also can be used to define single identifiers that are equivalent to expressions.

For example, you could use the #define directive to declare the following identifiers:

```
#define TRUE   1
#define FALSE  0
#define PI 3.1415
#define TAX 8.25
```

Example

```
#define FIVE 5
int main()
{
    printf("The number is %d", FIVE);
    return 0;
}
```

You should be familiar with this type of #define example, which has been used previously in this book. The lines cause the compiler to substitute the associated constant each time that the compiler encounters the identifier.

After you define an expression, you can use it as often as you like. By convention, C programmers use uppercase characters for #define identifiers. Uppercase makes it clear in a program that you are referring to a #define identifier rather than to a variable name. The compiler does not require this convention, however.

Following are examples of macro type #define statements:

```
#define AREA length * width
#define MESSAGE printf("this is a message")
```

The idea behind macros is the same as the #define statements with which you are already familiar. Whenever the preprocessor finds the identifier in the program, it swaps the identifier with the replacement string. In the first example, if you use the identifier AREA in your program, the preprocessor replaces it with the following string:

```
length * width
```

In the second example, if you use the identifier MESSAGE, the preprocessor replaces it with this string:

```
printf("this is a message")
```

It is important to understand that macros simply replace an identifier with a string of text. To define a standard error message, for example, you might code something like this:

```
#define MSG "ERROR:  THINGS AREN'T WORKING RIGHT\n"
  .
  .
  .
printf(MSG);
```

This code causes the compiler to substitute the string when it encounters the identifier MSG. Thus, the compiler reads the statement as follows:

```
printf("ERROR:  THINGS AREN'T WORKING RIGHT\n");
```

Caution

Macros are limited in that they cannot replace text if the identifier is found inside a string. For example, the statement

```
printf("MSG");
```

prints only the actual text—MSG—rather than the full text associated with the MSG identifier.

Macro definitions usually are placed at the beginning of a file or inside a header file. The macro definition can be accessed from its point of definition to the end of the file. The following rules apply to creating macros:

- The name of the macro must follow the rules for all identifiers in C. Most important, the macro name cannot contain spaces.

- The macro definition should not be terminated by a semicolon, unless you want to include the semicolon in your replacement string.

- Macros cannot be used inside quotation marks, as you saw earlier.

- Macro definitions usually are limited to a single line. However, the backslash character (\) can be used at the end of each line—except the last—to extend the macro definition to more than one line.

Using macros can save you time in a couple of ways. First, macros can save you coding time by making it easy to change constant values. Second, macros make your program easier to read.

Listing 8.1 is an example of a program that uses a macro definition. The program calculates the area of a rectangle, given the width and height.

Listing 8.1   A Program To Calculate the Area of a Rectangle, Using Macros

```
/***************************************************
   MACROS.C - Calculate area of rectangle.
***************************************************/

#include <stdio.h>

/* macro definition */
#define AREA length * width


int main()
{
   int length, width;

   printf("Enter length: ");
   scanf("%d", &length);

   printf("Enter width: ");
   scanf("%d", &width);

   printf("\nresulting area is %d\n", AREA);

   return 0;
}
```

Listing 8.1 (MACROS.C) contains the macro AREA, which represents the expression length * width. When the program is compiled, the expression length * width replaces the identifier AREA in the printf() function, so the printf() statement becomes

```
printf("\nresulting area is %d\n", length * width);
```

Notice that the string inside quotation marks is unaffected by the program. This happens for two reasons. First, the text inside strings cannot be replaced with macros. Second, the string is lowercase, and the macro is declared as uppercase. Remember that C is a case-sensitive language—this includes the C preprocessor.

Listing 8.2 is an example of a multiline macro, showing how multiline macros are defined by placing the backslash (\) character at the end of each line in the macro.

Listing 8.2   A Multiline Macro Definition

```
/**************************************************
   TRI.C - Use multiline macro to create triangle.
 **************************************************/

#include <stdio.h>

/* macro definition */
#define loop for(lines=1; lines<=n; lines++)      \
        {                                          \
        for(count=1; count<=n-lines; count++)     \
            putchar(' ');                          \
        for(count=1; count<=2*lines-1; count++)   \
            putchar('#');                          \
        printf("\n");                              \
            }


int main()
{

    int count, lines, n;

    printf("Enter number of lines: ");
    scanf("%d", &n);
    printf("\n");

    /* reference to macro */
    loop

    return 0;
}
```

When the program runs, it displays a triangle of pound signs with a height determined by the user. The program looks something like this when you run it:

```
Enter number of lines: 7

      #
     ###
    #####
   #######
  #########
 ###########
#############
```

The program demonstrates how you can put almost anything you want in a macro. The entire core loop of the program is in the macro definition.

Macro Parameters

You also can pass parameters to a macro; these parameters then can be used inside the macro. Several standard library functions—for example, putchar()—actually are macros in disguise. putchar() is a macro because it calls the putc() function with a pointer to the output device. You will find other macros defined in the standard header files.

To pass a parameter to a macro, list the parameter names in the declaration. You could declare a macro this way:

```
#define DISPLAY(i) printf("%d\n", i)
```

Then use it like this:

```
DISPLAY(3);
```

When you run the program, the result is

```
printf("%d\n", 3);
```

Thus, the parameter i is passed to the macro. The preprocessor then copies the i to the specified location in the macro declaration.

Undefining Macros

You can undefine a macro by using the #undef directive. The preprocessor directive removes any previous macro definition. After you undefine a macro, you can redefine it by using the #define preprocessor directive.

You could use code that looks something like this to redeclare the value of a definition:

```
#define MAXIMUM 1024
...
#undef MAXIMUM
...
#define MAXIMUM 512
```

The capability to undefine macros can be useful for large projects and for projects in which macros have to change.

The `#undef` preprocessor directive is handy in a situation in which you have several program files. The preprocessor checks each file to see whether a symbol has been defined. Later, the preprocessor checks for the symbol again— this time, you don't want the action carried out. You can use the `#undef` directive to undefine the symbol.

You have taken a good look at macro definitions. The next type of preprocessor directive that you examine is the error-generation directive.

Error Generation

You can cause the error-generation preprocessor directive to report an error condition to the programmer. The directive also forces the compiler to stop compilation.

The Preprocessor Directive

The preprocessor takes this form:

> `#error error-message`

The `error-message` does not appear in double quotation marks. When the preprocessor encounters this directive, it displays the following information and terminates compilation:

> `Error: filename linenumber`
> `Error directive: error-message`

The following code fragment is an example:

> `#error Please define program name`

When the preprocessor checks this line, it stops processing the file and displays the message `"Please define program name."`

This preprocessor directive is used for debugging. It also can be embedded in a preprocessor conditional directive that catches some undesirable compile-time condition. Suppose that you have source code that you want to compile for both DOS and UNIX environments. You first can check to see whether a symbol has been defined; then you can compile certain parts of the code, depending on which environment you are targeting.

The error-generation directive normally is used with conditional compilation, which is discussed in the following section.

Conditional Compilation

Several directives enable you to compile portions of your program's source code selectively. This process, called *conditional compilation*, is used widely in large programs that have several versions.

The Preliminaries

The general idea behind conditional compilation is that you include preprocessor directives in your code. These directives check for certain definitions. If the definitions are defined, the compiler compiles the code between the definition and the end of the conditional statement. If the condition evaluates to false, the compiler replaces it with blank lines, in effect skipping it.

You use the #if statement to test for an expression. Then use the #endif statement at the end of the block of code that is to be conditionally compiled.

Conditional Compilation

The general format of the #if precompiler directive is as follows:

```
#if expression
...
other C statements
...
#endif
```

If *expression* is true, the compiler skips the specified block of code. Otherwise (if *expression* is false), the compiler skips the code. See the following example:

```
#if __BORLANDC__
printf("This message is only displayed if compiling"
        "with the Borland compiler\n");
#endif
```

Listing 8.3 shows another example of conditional compilation.

Listing 8.3   An Example of Conditional Compilation

```
/***************************************************
   CONDIT.C - Example of conditional compilation.
 ***************************************************/

#define MAX 200

#include <stdio.h>

int main()
{
#if MAX > 100
    printf("compiled for numbers greater than 100\n");
#endif
    return 0;
}
```

When the program is compiled, it displays the message on-screen because MAX is greater than 100. The expression is evaluated at compile time. Therefore, the expression must contain identifiers that have been defined previously. The expression cannot use any program variables.

Much like the if statement in C, the preprocessor enables your program to have an else clause. The #else directive establishes an alternative if the #if statement fails. Listing 8.4 shows an expansion of listing 8.3.

Listing 8.4   Using the *#else* Directive in a Program

```
/***************************************************
   CONDIT2.C - Example of the #else directive.
 ***************************************************/

#define MAX 50

#include <stdio.h>

int main()
{

#if MAX > 100
    printf("compiled for numbers greater than 100\n");
#else
    printf("compiled for numbers less than 100\n");
#endif

    return 0;
}
```

This version of the program defines MAX to be 50. The preprocessor directive passes this code to the compiler only if MAX is greater than 100. Because the program defines MAX to be 50, that section of code is never compiled; instead, the code following the `#else` statement is compiled. The program uses the `#endif` to mark the end of the block.

There is yet another type of conditional compilation statement. This statement, called `#elif`, stands for *else if*. `#elif` enables you to create an if/else /if construction for multiple compilation options.

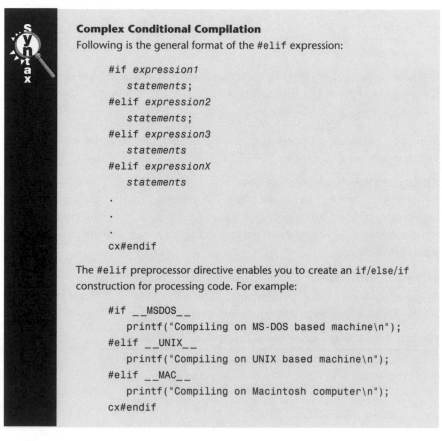

Complex Conditional Compilation

Following is the general format of the `#elif` expression:

```
#if expression1
    statements;
#elif expression2
    statements;
#elif expression3
    statements
#elif expressionX
    statements

    .

    .

    .

cx#endif
```

The `#elif` preprocessor directive enables you to create an if/else/if construction for processing code. For example:

```
#if __MSDOS__
    printf("Compiling on MS-DOS based machine\n");
#elif __UNIX__
    printf("Compiling on UNIX based machine\n");
#elif __MAC__
    printf("Compiling on Macintosh computer\n");
cx#endif
```

It is important to remember that if the expression is not valid, the code is not compiled. This is great for creating multiple versions of a program, each with different capabilities. If you sell two versions of your program—a professional version and a standard version—you could use conditional-compilation options to add the statements necessary for the professional version. Then, to compile your program for the standard version, you change one line, defining REGULAR instead of PROFESSIONAL.

Another use of preprocessor directives is to define different header files for the different computers on which you run your program. Then you can use conditional-compilation features to compile only certain parts of your program. For example:

```
#if defined (DOS)
#include "dos.h"
#elif defined(UNIX)
#include "unix.h"
#elif defined (MAC)
#include "mac.h"
#else
#include "default.h"
cx#endif
```

If you were using these lines on a DOS machine, you would have defined DOS somewhere earlier in the file with this line:

```
#define DOS
```

You can store specific information in each header file about the machine on which you want to compile.

These conditional-compilation features can make a program more portable. By changing a few key definitions at the beginning of a file, you can set up different values and include different files for different systems. This capability is a powerful aspect of the C programming language—one that most languages don't offer.

Using Conditional Compiling While Debugging

You can use conditional compilation to add extra code to your program while you are debugging it, as shown in listing 8.5.

Listing 8.5   Using Conditional Compiling To Debug

```
/******************************************
   ERROR.C - Error generation directives.
******************************************/
/* define this to enable debugging information*/
#define DEBUGGING

#include <stdio.h>

int main()
{
   int i;
   int total = 0;

   for (i=1; i<= 4; i++)
   {
      total = total + 2;
#ifdef DEBUGGING
      printf("i equals %d, total = %d\n", i, total);
#endif
   }
```

```
    printf("Total is %d\n", total);

    return 0;
}
```

Compiling and running the program as shown produces the following output:

```
i equals 1, total = 2
i equals 2, total = 4
i equals 3, total = 6
i equals 4, total = 8
Total is 8
```

If you omit the definition for DEBUGGING and recompile the program, however, the program displays only the final line. You can use this approach to help debug your programs. Define DEBUGGING in your program and use the #ifdef preprocessor directive heavily. You then display extra information on-screen that you can use to ensure that the program is compiling correctly.

When the program works correctly, you can remove the definition and recompile. The program is not larger because the preprocessor doesn't include the debugging code. By the time the compiler reaches the code, the compiler does not even know that the code exists.

Later, if you have to debug your code again, insert the DEBUGGING definition and recompile your program.

Testing for Errors

You can use the error-generation routines along with the conditional-compilation features to compile programs that check for certain values. Listing 8.6 shows how you can use this feature.

> **Note**
>
> The first line of code in the following program (#define BORLANDC) should not be typed on non-Borland compilers. That is how the #error directive is generated; it displays a message stating that the function is not available.

Listing 8.6 Example of Error Generation During Compilation

```
/*****************************************
   CHECKS.C - Producing error messages.
*****************************************/

#define BORLANDC
```

(continues)

Listing 8.6   Continued

```
/* Make sure you are using the*/
/* correct version of your compiler. */
#ifndef BORLANDC
#error Sorry, Borland C required to compile program
#endif

#include <stdio.h>


#include <conio.h>

int main()
{

    clrscr();
/* Clear screen using Borland C specific function. */

    return 0;

}
```

The program uses a function that is specific to the Borland C compiler. Therefore, the program uses the #ifndef statement at the beginning to ensure that the correct value is declared.

The #ifndef preprocessor directive checks to see whether a symbol has been defined. If the specified symbol has not been defined, the preprocessor executes the instructions up to an #endif instruction.

Although the simple example shows the definition and the test right after it, a more complex project probably would contain several files, and you could use the test in different locations.

Predefined Names

The ANSI C language contains five built-in macro names, which are described in table 8.1. Many compilers define additional macro names.

Table 8.1 Predefined Macro Names	
Name	**Description**
__LINE__	Contains the current source-code line number
__FILE__	Contains the name of the file being compiled
__DATE__	Contains the date when the program was compiled

Name	Description
_ _TIME_ _	Contains the time when the program was compiled
_ _STDC_ _	Specifies that the compiler is ANSI C-compliant

The _ _LINE_ _ macro points to the line in the source code that is being compiled. The _ _FILE_ _ macro contains the name of the file that is being compiled.

Two macros define when the source code is compiled. The _ _TIME_ _ macro contains a string indicating the time the compile took place. This time usually is the time at which the compilation began. The _ _DATE_ _ macro contains a string of the form mm/dd/yy, which is the date of the translation of the source file into object code. Following is a good example of using a predefined macro:

```
printf("Current line number is %d", __LINE__);
```

This code displays a message with the current line number of the source-code file.

The macro _ _STDC_ _ contains the constant 1. This constant means that the implementation of C confirms to the ANSI specification. If the constant is not defined, the compiler is not ANSI-compliant.

Line Control

The #line directive is used to change the line number and name of the current source file. Following is the basic format of the command:

```
#line number ["filename"]
```

number is any positive integer value, and the optional *filename* is any valid file identifier. The *number* is the number of the current source line, and the *filename* is the name of the source file. The #line preprocessor directive is used primarily for debugging purposes. Listing 8.7 shows how the directive is used.

> **Caution**
>
> If no source file is defined in *filename,* the compiler issues a warning and does not accept your code.

Listing 8.7   Use of the *#line* Directive

```
/**************************************************
   LINE.C - Display current line number.
 **************************************************/

#include <stdio.h>

int main()
{
    printf("line number: %d\n", __LINE__);
    printf("file name: %s\n", __FILE__);

#line 100 "newfile"

    printf("line number: %d\n", __LINE__);
    printf("file name: %s\n", __FILE__);


    return 0;
}
```

The #line directive actually changes the value of the __LINE__ and __FILE__ predefined names that you learned earlier.

Summary

This chapter examined the C preprocessor. You learned how to use the pre-processor to create macro definitions and for error generation, line control, and conditional compilation. In particular, this chapter covered the following points:

- *File inclusion* enables a program to insert the contents of a separate file at a specific point in a program.

- If you include angle brackets around your include file, the preprocessor looks for the included file at a predetermined location. If you enclose the file name in quotation marks, the preprocessor looks for the file in the current directory.

- Header files usually are reserved for function prototypes, variable declarations, and other preprocessor directives. Header files usually don't include source code.

- Macros are used in a program to replace an identifier with a specified string of characters. The preprocessor replaces the identifiers with the characters, so the C compiler does not know that the replacement is occurring.

■ A limitation of macros is that a macro identifier cannot appear inside a string (within double quotation marks).

■ To pass a parameter to a macro, you list the parameter names in the macro declaration.

■ Macros can be undefined with the `#undef` preprocessor directive. When this directive is used, any previous macro definition is erased.

■ You can cause the preprocessor to abort processing and display a message by using the `#error` preprocessor directive.

■ *Conditional compilation* enables you to control the portions of your program's source code that should be compiled.

Chapter 9

Using Pointers

Although pointers are used in other programming languages, such as BASIC and Pascal, they are hidden from the programmer and are not essential to using the language. The understanding and correct use of pointers are critical to the creation of practically every large C program.

Although pointers are one of C's strongest features, they also can be one of the most dangerous features. Uninitialized pointers can easily cause a system crash. Also, it is easy to use pointers incorrectly, causing program errors that are difficult to track down. Therefore, be sure to learn the basics presented in this chapter.

About Pointers

A *pointer* is a special type of variable that points to a specific location in memory. A pointer represents the location (rather than the value) of a variable. Most often, the location is the address of another variable in memory, although a pointer can refer to any memory location. Typically, a pointer points to a part of memory where a value is stored or where one is to be stored.

The reasons for using pointers include:

- Pointers provide a method by which functions can modify their calling arguments. Pointers can be used to pass more than one piece of information back and forth between a function and the place in the code from which it is called.

- Pointers are used to support dynamic memory allocation. You can actually create variables as your program is running.

- Pointer operations provide increased efficiency when they are substituted for accessing arrays. The pointer provides an alternative method of accessing individual array elements.

Pointers are an important part of the power of the C programming language.

Declaring Pointers

To declare a pointer, you must use a special *pointer declaration* to inform the compiler that you are about to declare a pointer variable.

Because different data types require different amounts of memory, a pointer declaration must include a specification of the data type to which it refers. You make this specification by defining a pointer that points to a specific data type.

Declaring Pointers

The general syntax for declaring a pointer variable is as follows:

```
datatype *name;
```

datatype is any valid C data type (`int`, `char`, `float`, and so on), and *name* is the name of the pointer variable. The data type defines the type of variable to which the pointer can point. The asterisk (*) is called the *indirection operator*. When this operator follows a data type, it translates to "pointer to" and indicates that the pointer points to a variable of the indicated type.

The following statements declare pointer variables:

```
char *a;
int *i, *begin;
```

The first statement declares one character pointer, and the second declares two integer pointers. After a pointer is declared, but before it has been assigned a value, it contains an unknown value.

Caution

Don't use a pointer before giving it a value, because you probably will crash your program. If you use a pointer before giving it a value, you are accessing an *uninitialized pointer*.

The C language has a convention in which a pointer that is pointing nowhere is set to equal the constant NULL. The NULL constant is a value that signifies to the compiler that the pointer points to nothing (it is equal to zero). The fact that a pointer is equal to NULL, however, does not mean you cannot use it; the compiler still enables you to use the pointer. But a NULL pointer can cause your program to crash at run time.

Pointer Operators

Two special operators work with pointers: & and *. The & operator is the *address operator,* which evaluates the address of a pointer variable.

Using the Pointer Operators

Following is the general format for using the pointer operators:

```
address = &ch;
```

This code places the memory address of the variable ch in the pointer variable address. The variable *address* represents ch's memory location, not its actual value; the memory location has nothing to do with the value of the variable. You can think of the job of the & operator as that of returning the address of the variable that it precedes.

The other pointer operator is *; its job is to return the value of the variable located at an address. For example, if *address* contains the memory location of the variable ch (as shown above), the statement:

```
contents = *address;
```

places the value of ch in the variable named *contents*. If ch originally stored the character 'Q', *contents* is equal to the character 'Q' because that is the value stored at location &ch. A verbal translation of the * operator is "variable pointed to by...". Following is an example:

```
result = &foo;
```

This statement assigns the address of the variable foo to the variable result.

What makes pointer notation difficult is that the asterisk is used both to declare a variable and to reference the value to which the pointer points. The asterisk also is used for multiplication. Don't worry—the compiler can tell when to perform the appropriate action. The notation makes it a little harder for humans to remember. After you use pointer notation for a while, it becomes easier and eventually becomes second nature.

Using Pointers

Listing 9.1 (VARADDR.C) demonstrates how to return the address of a variable by using the & operator.

Listing 9.1   Demonstrates How To Find a Variable's Address

```
/***************************************
   VARADDR.C - Address of variables.
***************************************/
```

(continues)

Listing 9.1 Continued

```c
#include <stdio.h>

int main()
{
    int var1 = 12;
    int var2 = 13;
    int var3 = 14;

    printf("Address of var1: %X\n", &var1);
    printf("Address of var2: %X\n", &var2);
    printf("Address of var3: %X\n", &var3);

    return 0;
}
```

This simple program defines three integer variables and initializes them to the values 12, 13, and 14. The program then prints the addresses of the variables. Notice that you need not declare a variable as a pointer to use the & operator. The variable is not required because all variables take up memory and the & operator returns the memory location of a variable.

The actual addresses of your variables depend on many factors, including the amount of memory available, the operating system, and whether any other programs are currently running. This purpose of listing 9.1 is to show you that a memory address is different from the contents of a variable.

Listing 9.2 illustrates the relationship between two integer variables, their corresponding addresses, and their associated pointers.

Listing 9.2 The Use of Pointers

```c
/************************************************
   PTR1.C - Shows the use of pointer operations.
 ************************************************/

#include <stdio.h>

int main()
{
    int a, b;   /* Integer variables     */
    int *pa;    /* Pointer to an integer */
    int *pb;    /* Pointer to an integer */

    a = 9;      /* Assign 9 to variable a */
    pa = &a;    /* Assign address of a to pa */
    b = *pa;    /* Assign value of a to b */
    pb = &b;    /* Assign address of b to pb */

    printf("Results are\n\n");

    printf("a=%d    &a=%X    pa=%x     *pa=%d\n",
```

```
           a, &a, pa, *pa);
    printf("b=%d    &b=%X    pb=%x      *pb=%d\n",
           b, &b, pb, *pb);

    return 0;
}
```

Notice that pa is a pointer to a and that pb is a pointer to b. Therefore, pa represents the address of a, and pb represents the address of b. The printf() statements illustrate the values of a and b and their associated values: *pa and *pb.

Running the program results in the following output:

```
Results are

a=9    &a=FFF4    pa=fff4    *pa=9
b=9    &b=FFF2    pb=fff2    *pb=9
```

Memory addresses most likely are different on your computer. In the first line, you see that a represents the value 9, as specified in the declaration. The address of a is determined by the compiler. The pointer pa is assigned this value; therefore, pa represents the same address. Finally, the value to which pa points (*pa) is 9, as you would expect.

Similarly, the second line shows that b also represents the value 9. This is expected because you assigned the value *pa to b. The address of b and the value of pb are the same. Notice that a and b have different addresses. Finally, notice that the value to which pb points is 9.

Returning Data from Functions

When you learned about functions in Chapter 7, "Modular Programming with Functions," you learned that you can return a single value to the calling program from a function by using the return statement. This transfer of a single piece of information can be rather limiting at times. Pointers, however, enable you to return more than one value from a function.

Pointers often are passed to a function as arguments. This procedure enables the function to directly access data items in the calling portion of the program, to alter the data items, and then to return the items to the calling portion of the program in an altered form.

Usually, when a parameter or argument is passed to a function, it is passed *by value*. When an argument is passed by value, a copy of the data item is passed to the function. Thus, any alterations made in the arguments of the function are not returned to the calling program.

When an argument is passed *by reference,* however, the address of a data item is passed to the function. The contents of that address can be accessed, and the values stored in the address can be modified in the function. These changes occur at the memory location of the variables.

Passing Pointers to Functions

Listing 9.3 illustrates the difference between ordinary arguments (passed by value) and pointer arguments (passed by reference).

Listing 9.3   An Example of Passing by Value and by Reference

```
/****************************************************
   FUNCTION.C - Difference between function call
                by value and by reference.
 ****************************************************/

#include <stdio.h>

/* Function declarations */
void first_function(int a, int b);
void second_function(int *pa, int *pb);

int main()
{
   int x = 0;
   int y = 0;

   printf("Before calling first_function, "
       "x=%d,   y=%d\n", x, y);

   first_function(x,y);

   printf("After calling first_function, "
       "x=%d,   y=%d\n\n", x, y);

   printf("Before calling second_function, "
       "x=%d,   y=%d\n", x, y);

   second_function(&x, &y);

   printf("After calling second_function, "
       "x=%d,   y=%d\n", x, y);

   return 0;
}

void first_function(int a, int b)
{
   a = 1;
   b = 1;
   printf("Inside first_function, "
       "a=%d b=%d \n", a,b);
}

void second_function(int *pa, int *pb)
```

```
{
    *pa = 2;
    *pb = 2;
    printf("Inside second_function, "
        "*a=%d, *b=%d\n", *pa, *pb);
}
```

The output of this program should look something like this:

```
Before calling first_function, x=0,  y=0
Inside first_function, a=1   b=1
After calling first_function, x=0,  y=0

Before calling second_function, x=0,  y=0
Inside second_function, *a=2, *b=2
After calling second_function, x=2,  y=2
```

The program contains two functions. The first function receives two integer variables as arguments. These variables originally have a value of 0 and receive a value of 1 inside the first function.

The values of the original variables do not change when the program returns to main(), because the arguments were passed by value.

> **Note**
>
> When arguments are passed by value, any changes made in the function's arguments are local in the function in which the change occurred.

The second function receives two pointers to integer variables as its arguments and is called as follows:

```
second_function(&x, &y);
```

The addresses are provided by the calling program, using the & operator. Control is passed to the function along with the addresses of the two variables.

The arguments in the function are identified as pointers by the asterisks that appear in the function's argument declaration, as follows:

```
void second_function(int *pa, int *pb)
```

In the second function, the contents of the pointer addresses are assigned the value of 2. Because the addresses are recognized in both the function and in main(), the values are changed in the main program as well as inside the function.

Library Functions and Pointers

As you have seen, some C library functions accept pointers as parameters. The one you have seen so far is scanf(), which is used to get input from the keyboard. For example:

```
char str[99];
scanf("%s", &str);
```

In this example, the & operator passes the address of the first element in the character array str to the scanf() function. The scanf() function gets the keystrokes from the user and returns them in the variable str.

Pointers and Strings

In C, character pointers are used quite often. In fact, character pointers are, in essence, an extension of character arrays. Take a look at listing 9.4.

Listing 9.4   String and Pointer Notation

```
/**************************************************
    PTR2.C - Pointers and strings.
 **************************************************/

#include <stdio.h>

int main()
{
   char *a;

   a = "Hello, World!";

   printf("%s\n", a);

   return 0;
}
```

A pointer variable is declared in the program. When you declare the pointer variable, it is available to point at a specific location in memory. To make proper use of it, you assign the string "Hello, World!" to the variable. The C compiler automatically adds a terminating \0 character to the string. The constant in quotation marks actually is written into the program, and when the program runs, the computer allocates a place in memory to store the constant. The pointer a does not equal the string. Instead, the pointer points to where the computer has stored the constant.

The output of the program displays the contents of the string. The printf() function outputs the string until it reaches the terminating \0 that is appended to the string automatically.

To clarify the concept, study listing 9.5, which is a modification of listing 9.4.

Listing 9.5   A Second Example of Using Pointers and Strings

```
/****************************************************
   PTR3.C - More about pointers and strings.
****************************************************/

#include <stdio.h>

int main()
{
   char *a;

   a = "Hello, World!";

   printf("%s\n", a);
   printf("%c\n", *a);

   return 0;
}
```

This program shows some of the notation used with pointers and character arrays. The first `printf()` function displays the full string, whereas the second `printf()` function displays the single character H.

The pointer is declared and first points to the beginning of the string `"Hello, World!"` in memory. The first `printf()` function call prints the string to which a points. The second `printf()` function call displays the letter H, the initial character to which `*a` points.

Using a pointer with the `*` operator indicates that the program has to read the memory of one element in the string. The `*a` uses the asterisk as the indirection operator to return the single character to which a points.

Character Arrays

As you recall from Chapter 3, "Variables and Operators," C has no specific string data type. Instead, you have to define and use character arrays to represent groups of characters. You probably are thinking that there must be some method of accessing these character arrays with pointers. You're right. Listing 9.6 shows you how to access character arrays with pointers.

Listing 9.6   Character Arrays and Pointers

```
/****************************************************
   PTR4.C - Pointers and character arrays.
****************************************************/

#include <stdio.h>

int main()
{
```

(continues)

Listing 9.6   Continued

```
    char *a, *c;
    char b[100] = "Crash Course in C";

    a = "Hello, World!";
    c = b;

    printf("a is %s\n", a);
    printf("b is %s\n", b);
    printf("c is %s\n", c);

    c = a;
    printf("c is now: %s\n", c);

    return 0;
}
```

This program creates two character pointers (*a and *c) and one character array (b). The output of the program looks like this:

```
a is Hello, World!
b is Crash Course in C
c is Crash Course in C
c is now: Hello, World!
```

You declare the character array to be 100 elements long (to give yourself breathing space) and assign to it the string "Crash Course in C". You then assign a to point to the beginning of the second string. Next, you assign c to point to the beginning of b.

You then display what each variable points to by making c equal a, using this simple assignment statement:

```
c = a;
```

You then display what c points to, showing that it is equal to the first string constant. Now you can see the relationship between character pointers and character arrays.

Moving Through Memory

Although you cannot perform any sort of regular arithmetic operations with pointers, you can use the increment and decrement arithmetic operator with pointers. Pointers enable you to cycle through each element in an array, as you can see in listing 9.7.

Listing 9.7   Moving Through Memory with Pointers

```
/**************************************************
   PTR5.C - Cycling through memory with pointers.
 **************************************************/
```

```
#include <stdio.h>

int main()
{
   char *a;

   a = "Just do it";

   while (*a != '\0')
   {
      printf("%c\n", *a);
      *a++;
   }

   return 0;
}
```

The preceding example actually counts through each element of a character array. Remember that the statement *a points to the first character in the array. By using the statement

```
*a++
```

you actually move the pointer so that it points to the second element in the string. Another *a++ counts to the third element, and so on, until you reach the end of the string.

Running the program prints the following letters on the output screen:

```
J
u
s
t

d
o

i
t
```

Each character in the string is accessed individually, displayed, and then followed by a line feed. The loop continues until it locates the end of the string (\0).

Each time a pointer is incremented, it points to the memory location of the element after the pointer. Each time a pointer is decremented, it points to the location of the preceding element.

In an example of a pointer to the character array, the pointer is incremented by one byte each time. All other pointers, however, increase or decrease by the length of the data type to which they point.

For an example, study the difference between one-byte characters and two-byte integers. When a character pointer is incremented, it increases by one. When an integer pointer is incremented, however, it actually increases by two (because an integer is stored in two bytes).

You also can use pointers to add or subtract integer values with pointers. For example, the expressions

```
a++;
a = a+1;
```

are the same. They both increment, by one, the location to which a points. You can increase the incrementation to five with this statement:

```
a = a+5;
```

Pointers and One-Dimensional Arrays

As you have seen, there is a close relationship between pointers and arrays. An array name actually is a pointer to the first element in the array. Therefore, if you have the declaration

```
arr[99];
```

the address of the first array element can be expressed as either

```
arr
```

or

```
&arr[0];
```

The address of the second array element can be written as either

```
&arr[1]
```

or

```
(arr+1)
```

This means that there actually are two different ways to refer to the address of an array element, as follows:

- You can write the actual array element, preceded by an ampersand (&).

- You can write an expression in which the subscript is added to the array name.

Listing 9.8 shows the methods you can use to access the array elements.

Listing 9.8 How To Use Pointers with One-Dimensional Arrays

```c
/***********************************************
  PTRARR.C - Using pointers with arrays.
 ***********************************************/

#include <stdio.h>

int main()
{
    int arr[3] = {11, 22, 33};

    printf("address of first array element "
        "(arr) %d\n", arr);
    printf("address of first array element "
        "(&arr[0]) %d\n", &arr[0]);

    printf("address of second array element "
        " (arr+1) %d\n", (arr + 1) );
    printf("address of second array element "
        "(&arr[1])  %d\n", &arr[1]);

    printf("contents of arr[0] is %d\n", arr[0]);
    printf("contents of arr[1] is %d\n", arr[1]);

    return 0;
}
```

The output of listing 9.8 is similar to this:

```
address of first array element (arr) -16
address of first array element (&arr[0]) -16
address of second array element (arr+1) -14
address of second array element (&arr[1]) -14
contents of arr[0] is 11
contents of arr[1] is 22
```

Note

The output of listing 9.8 may look different on your system, depending on the type of machine you are using.

The program demonstrates the two methods of accessing the addresses of an array.

An alternate form of specifying the first array element is

```
*(arr + 1)
```

This method is equivalent to

```
(arr+1)
```

and the two terms are interchangeable. The choice depends on your own preference. Listing 9.9 illustrates the relationship between array elements and their addresses.

Listing 9.9   Another Method of Accessing Array Elements

```
/****************************************************
   PTRARR2.C - Another method of accessing arrays.
 ****************************************************/

#include <stdio.h>

int main()
{
    int arr[10] = { 11, 22, 33, 44, 55, 66,
                77, 88, 99, 111 };
    int index;

    for (index=0; index<10; index++)
       printf("index= %d, arr[index]= %d, "
              "*(arr+index)= %d, &arr[index]= %d,"
              "arr+index= %d\n", index, arr[index],
              *(arr+index), &arr[index],
              arr+index);

    return 0;
}
```

The program displays a table showing how to access array elements with pointers. The capability to access array elements through pointer notation provides great flexibility in C.

Although formatted differently here, for page-width reasons, the table has the following output:

```
index= 0, arr[index]= 11, *(arr+index)= 11,
                  &arr[index]= -30,arr+index= -30
index= 1, arr[index]= 22, *(arr+index)= 22,
                  &arr[index]= -28,arr+index= -28
index= 2, arr[index]= 33, *(arr+index)= 33,
                  &arr[index]= -26,arr+index= -26
index= 3, arr[index]= 44, *(arr+index)= 44,
                  &arr[index]= -24,arr+index= -24
index= 4, arr[index]= 55, *(arr+index)= 55,
                  &arr[index]= -22,arr+index= -22
index= 5, arr[index]= 66, *(arr+index)= 66,
                  &arr[index]= -20,arr+index= -20
index= 6, arr[index]= 77, *(arr+index)= 77,
                  &arr[index]= -18,arr+index= -18
index= 7, arr[index]= 88, *(arr+index)= 88,
                  &arr[index]= -16,arr+index= -16
index= 8, arr[index]= 99, *(arr+index)= 99,
                  &arr[index]= -14,arr+index= -14
index= 9, arr[index]= 111, *(arr+index)= 111,
                  &arr[index]= -12,arr+index= -12
```

This table shows the result of using each different method of accessing the array elements.

Dynamic-Memory Allocation

All the data structures you have examined so far have been *static* data structures, meaning that the C compiler allocates memory for the variables when they are declared. The variables then occupy memory space throughout the execution of the program.

Static memory allocation is simple to manage but somewhat inflexible. For example, when you create an array, you must tell C how large the array should be when you declare it. This information is required so that the correct amount of memory is available to your program when it executes. If you allocate too little space to an array, your program will crash. If you use fewer array elements than the number you declared, a certain amount of memory is left unused and, therefore, wasted.

Caution

Be careful not to allocate too little space for your array when you use static memory allocation. If you do so (by accessing elements beyond the maximum size of the array), your program will crash.

The opposite of static data structures are *dynamic* data structures. The memory for these data structures is allocated as the program is executed; thus, a dynamic data structure can grow as needed. Furthermore, if you allocate the memory space and then find that you don't need it anymore, the dynamic data structure can shrink, releasing memory for use by other data.

Note

At first glance, it may not seem awkward to refer to a variable by using a pointer. By using pointers, however, you can achieve incredible power in programming. Pointers enable you to create variables while a program is executing. In fact, the `malloc()` and `calloc()` functions enable you to define a variable that is not part of any variable declaration. To put it another way, these functions enable you to create variables and then destroy them during the execution of your program. When you use pointers, you can create dynamic data structures that can grow or shrink as your program executes.

The *malloc( )* and *calloc( )* Functions

Pointers can point to any area of memory. Usually, pointers are aimed at portions of memory in which data is set aside. C provides functions that enable a pointer to point to an area of memory that is set aside specifically for new data.

You can instruct the system to set aside a certain area of memory that can later be accessed with a pointer. You simply specify how many bytes of storage space are required; the compiler determines where the data is to be stored.

The functions that form the C compiler's dynamic-memory-allocation system include malloc() and calloc(). These functions are part of the standard C language function library and usually are supported by every C compiler. To use them, you must include the header file ALLOC.H at the beginning of your program, as follows:

```
#include <alloc.h>
```

The malloc() function allocates a block of memory. The calloc() function does the same thing, but it first clears each memory location to 0. You use the calloc() function in place of malloc() if you must initialize the memory space to 0 before you use it.

Both functions take a single integer parameter declaring how much memory you want to allocate. The function returns a pointer to the first byte of memory that was allocated. If not enough memory is available, the functions return NULL.

To create an integer variable, for example, use the following statement:

```
p = (int *)malloc (sizeof (int)));
  /* pointer to an int */
```

This function is complicated, so you should examine each part. First, notice the sizeof(int) expression; this is the parameter passed to the malloc() function. The malloc() function allocates the amount of space that is passed from the sizeof() function and returns a pointer to the memory. The sizeof() function is used to return the amount of bytes required for an integer.

You then use the expression (int *) before the malloc() function. This expression is called a *typecast*—it informs the compiler that you want to interpret the return address of malloc() as a pointer to an integer. The malloc() function does not indicate what data type its return value is, which is why you must inform the compiler what data type you are using. Finally, you assign the address of the new integer to the pointer p.

After you use the `malloc()` statement, you can use `*p` as you would any other integer variable. You can assign it a value or return a value to it from another function, as follows:

```
*p = 1995;
scanf("%d", p);
```

During the execution of your program, you can use the preceding method to create as many variables as you need. Following are other examples of dynamic-memory allocation:

```
pd = (double *)malloc (sizeof (double));
/* pointer to a double */
pc = (char *)malloc (sizeof (char));
/* pointer to a char */
```

To access the variables, you use the following statement:

```
*pd = 3.14;
*pc = 'P';
```

The *free( )* Function

The opposite of the `malloc()` and `calloc()` functions is the `free()` function, which returns previously allocated memory to the system. The `free()` function attempts to free a block of allocated memory, thereby making it available for other purposes.

Using the *free( )* Function

Following is the general format of the `free()` function:

```
free(p);
```

p is the pointer to a previously allocated block of memory. The compiler actually keeps an internal list where the memory was allocated; therefore, it frees the location you refer to with the pointer that you pass to the function. The following example illustrates `free()`:

```
#include <alloc.h>

int main()
{
    char *mem;

    mem = (char*)malloc(10);

    free(mem);
    return 0;
}
```

> **Caution**
>
> It is important to call the `free()` function with a valid argument, because passing invalid arguments causes the computer to scramble the memory-block list.

Listing 9.10 is an example of dynamic-memory allocation.

> **Note**
>
> Borland C and Microsoft C use different header files to prototype their memory-allocation functions. If you use Borland C/C++, make sure that you include the ALLOC.H header file; if you use Microsoft's Visual C/C++, make sure that you include the MALLOC.H header file. The following listing is written for Borland C, so if you are using Microsoft's Visual C/C++, change the include file to MALLOC.H.

Listing 9.10   An Example of Dynamic-Memory Allocation

```c
/***************************************************
  MEMALLOC.C - Dynamic-memory allocation.
***************************************************/

#include <stdio.h>
#include <alloc.h>

int main()
{
   int counter, number, temp;
   int *arr;

   printf("How many numbers do you want to store?");
   scanf("%d", &number);

   arr = (int *) malloc(number * sizeof(int));
                         /* Allocate memory */

   printf("Enter numbers\n");
   for (counter=0; counter<number; counter++)
   {
      printf("  Enter number %d: ", counter+1);
      scanf("%d", &temp);
      arr[counter] = temp;
   }

   printf("\nNumbers are\n");
   for (counter=0; counter<number; counter++)
                         /* Display numbers */
      printf("  Number %d is %d\n",
             counter+1, arr[counter]);

   free(arr);

   return 0;
}
```

The program asks the user how many numbers should be stored. The program then allocates the memory space and prompts the user for each number. Finally, the program displays the numbers on-screen and frees the memory so that it can be used for other purposes.

Sample output looks like this:

```
How many numbers do you want to store? 4
Enter numbers
  Enter number 1: 44
  Enter number 2: 33
  Enter number 3: 22
  Enter number 4: 11

Numbers are
  Number 1 is 44
  Number 2 is 33
  Number 3 is 22
  Number 4 is 11
```

The memory allocation is performed with the following statement:

```
arr = (int *) malloc(number * sizeof(int));
```

The malloc() function is passed the number of bytes to be allocated. A typecast sets *arr* to point to the memory returned by the function.

A loop is created that prompts for each number. The number first is stored in the variable temp. The allocated memory can be accessed just like an array, and the element in the array is assigned the value that was stored in the temporary variable. The expression arr still points to the first element in the array. The following statements swap between the temporary variable and the dynamic-memory locations:

```
scanf("%d", &temp);
arr[counter] = temp;
```

After the elements are redisplayed on-screen, the free() function is used so that the memory can be used for another purpose. In this program, you need not use free(), because when the program terminates, memory is reallocated to the system anyway. It is good practice, however, to use the free() function to return memory to the system.

Pointers and Multidimensional Arrays

Because a one-dimensional array can be accessed with pointers, it is reasonable to expect that multidimensional arrays also can be represented with pointer notation. This certainly is true.

Two-Dimensional Array Declarations

A two-dimensional array actually is a collection of one-dimensional arrays. Therefore, you can define a two-dimensional array as a pointer to a group of one-dimensional arrays.

Declaring Two-Dimensional Array Pointers

The general format of a two-dimensional array is

```
datatype *pointername[expression2];
```

instead of

```
datatype arrayname[expression1][expression2];
```

datatype refers to the data type of the array, *pointername* is the name of the pointer variable, *arrayname* is the corresponding array name, and *expression1* and *expression2* are positive integer expressions that indicate the maximum number of array elements associated with the array.

To declare a two-dimensional array with five rows and ten columns, use one of the following equivalent statements:

```
int arr[5][10];
int (*arr)[10];
```

The first statement declares arr to be a two-dimensional array with five rows and ten columns. The second statement declares arr to be a pointer to a group of one-dimensional, ten-element arrays. Therefore arr points to the first ten-element array, which actually is the first row (row 0) of the original two-dimensional array. Then (arr+1) points to the second ten-element array, and so on.

Multidimensional Array Declarations

You can declare multidimensional array pointers much the same way that you declare two-dimensional array pointers.

Declaring Multidimensional Array Pointers

The general format of a multidimensional array declared with pointer notation is

```
datatype (*pointername)[expression1]
    [expression2]...[expressionN];
```

The following example declares a pointer to a character array that is 10x5020 elements:

```
char (*ptr)[10][5][20];
```

An individual array element in a multidimensional array can be accessed by using the indirection operator repeatedly. Usually, however, this procedure is more tedious than the regular method of accessing array elements.

Summary

This chapter introduced pointers and covered some of the ways in which pointers are used. In particular, the chapter covered the following topics:

- A *pointer* is a special type of variable that points to a specific location in memory. The pointer represents a memory location rather than a value.

- Pointers are used to (1) provide a method by which functions can pass data, (2) enable dynamic data allocation, and (3) provide increased efficiency in accessing array elements.

- A *pointer declaration* consists of a base data type, an asterisk (*), and the variable name.

- Two special pointer operators are included with the C programming language: & and *. The & operator returns the memory address of its operand. The * operator complements the & operator; it returns the value of the variable located at an address.

- When parameters are passed to a function, the parameters are passed *by value*. When data is passed by value, a copy of the data item is passed to the function. When pointers are passed between functions, the parameters are passed *by reference,* whereby the actual parameters passed to the function can be accessed and changed.

■ You can access strings with pointers by using the & and * operators. You can use two methods to access array elements. If *x* is declared a one-dimensional array, the first element of the array can be accessed as either &x[0] or simply as x. The address of the second array element can be written as &x[1] or x+1.

■ *Static data structures* are defined when you write your program and are available throughout the execution of your program. When a static variable is declared to be a specific size, that size cannot change during program execution.

■ *Dynamic data structures* are variables that can be allocated as the program is executed. A dynamic data structure can grow as required by your program. When the variable is not needed any longer, the memory that it occupies can be released for use by other variables.

■ The malloc() *and* calloc() functions are used to allocate memory and to return a pointer to the memory location. The big difference between these functions is that calloc() clears the allocated memory to 0 before returning a pointer to the memory.

■ The free() function returns to the system memory previously allocated with the malloc() or calloc() function.

■ Memory that is dynamically allocated is accessed through the use of brackets, similar to the way that you access an array.

■ Multidimensional arrays can be accessed with pointers in the same way that one-dimensional arrays are accessed.

Chapter 10

Advanced Data Structures

You learned about the basic types of variables in Chapter 3, "Variables and Operators." This chapter discusses some of the more advanced data structures available in the C programming language.

A *data structure* is a collection of data organized in a particular way. You know about the fundamental data types, including int, char, double, float, and long double. The basic data types involve only a single piece of information. You have seen how arrays combine groups of related data. This chapter looks at data structures that combine several different types of variables. You learn about C's struct type, data unions, and other topics. At the end of the chapter, you learn about some of the string-manipulation functions that are available in the standard C library.

Using Structures

Arrays are an excellent way to store data. However, they are limited because each element of an array must be of the same data type, and data doesn't always come bundled in similar packages. The C programming language provides a data structure that enables you to combine information about different types of data.

Suppose that you decide to computerize your address book. Although many programs can do this for you, you prefer to write your own program. In your simplified address book, the data you have for each person includes a name, address, city, state, ZIP code, and phone number.

You can't use an array to store these values, because they include both numbers and strings. Structures are the best method of storing these data items. Each element of a structure does not have to be the same type—and in most cases, the elements are *not* the same type.

Declaring Structures

Use the following general format to declare structures:

```
struct name
{
    datatype element1;
    datatype element2;
        .
        .
        .
    datatype elementX;
};
```

A structure actually is a data type with a format defined by the programmer. The preceding description shows how to define the structure to the compiler. When the structure is declared, you must create a variable declaration, which associates a symbolic *name* with the structure, as follows:

```
struct name uniquename;
```

You must use the keyword `struct`, followed by the name of the structure. The variable *name* (in this case, *uniquename*) contains the actual type you gave to the variable.

Each element of the structure is accessed by using the base name of the variable, a period, then the name of the element. Following is an example:

```
name.element1
name.element2
name.elementX
```

Listing 10.1 further demonstrates the process of defining, declaring, and using structures.

Listing 10.1   An Example of Using Structures

```
/*******************************************
  STRUCT.C - Using structures.
*******************************************/

#include <stdio.h>

struct astruct
            /* Structure definition  */
{
   int number;
   float amount;
```

```
        char let;
    };

    int main()
    {
        struct astruct thisstruct;
                    /* Variable declaration  */

        thisstruct.number  = 99;
                    /* Assignment statements  */
        thisstruct.amount  = 29.95;
        thisstruct.let     = 'P';

        printf("value thisstruct.number = %d\n",
               thisstruct.number);
        printf("value thisstruct.amount = %f\n",
               thisstruct.amount);
        printf("value thisstruct.let    = %c\n",
               thisstruct.let);

        return 0;
    }
```

The first part of the program declares the structure, as follows:

```
    struct astruct
    {
        int number;
        float amount;
        char let;
    };
```

This section of code declares a structure with three elements. The first element is of type integer (int) and is named number. The second element is type floating-point (float) and is named amount. The last element is a character type (char) and is named let. The preceding lines declare only what the structure type will be; they do not reserve memory for the structure. The following lines reserve memory for the structure:

```
    struct astruct thisstruct;
```

Notice the use of the keyword struct, which is followed by the structure name and the name of the variable. C permits a shortcut definition of a structure, including the definition and variable declaration. For the preceding program, the shortcut looks like this:

```
    struct astruct
    {
        int number;
        float amount;
        char let;
    } thisstruct;
```

This section of code enables you to accomplish the definition and declaration in one step.

To access structure elements, use the dot operator, as follows:

```
thisstruct.number = 99;
thisstruct.amount = 29.95;
thisstruct.let = 'P';
```

These statements are assignment statements. You can access each element in the structure by using dot notation. When the contents of the elements are displayed on-screen, you again use the dot operator to access each structure element.

In this section, you learned that structures are an extremely convenient method of storing unrelated data and often are used in large programs. Now you are ready to learn about a related subject: arrays of structures.

Arrays of Structures

Just as you can have arrays of integers, arrays of characters, and arrays of floating-point numbers, you also can have arrays of structures. First, you have to declare the structure, as you normally do.

Declaring Arrays of Structures

Following is an example of an array of a structure:

```
struct astruct
{
    int first;
    char second;
    float third;
};
```

You then declare the array. The array declaration looks like this:

```
struct astruct mystructarr[5];
```

Notice that the structure-array declaration is similar to a regular array declaration. Referencing the structure-array elements, however, is a little trickier. Add the array element immediately after the variable name. The dot operator follows. Finally, you add the field name. Some examples follow:

```
mystructarr[1].first = 2;
mystructarr[4].third = 7.68;
mystructarr[3].second = 'p';
```

Listing 10.2 shows a program that uses an array of structures.

Listing 10.2   Using an Array of Structures

```
/***************************************************
   STRUCTA.C - Using an array of structures.
 ***************************************************/
#include <stdio.h>
#include <stdlib.h>
#define DIM 3
/* The following is required with
   Borland C so the compiler will
   correctly link floating-point
   libraries.  */

#ifdef __BORLANDC__
extern void _floatconvert();
#pragma extref _floatconvert
#endif

struct data
{
   int numb;
   float amount;
   char name[25];
};


int main()
{
   struct data thisdata[DIM];
   int count;

   for (count=0; count<DIM; count++)
   {
      printf("\nData for element # %d\n", count+1);

      printf("Enter number: ");
      scanf("%d", &thisdata[count].numb);

      printf("Enter Amount: ");
      scanf("%f", &thisdata[count].amount);

      printf("Enter Name: ");
      scanf("%s", &thisdata[count].name);
   }

   printf("\n\n");

   for (count=0; count<DIM; count++)
   {
      printf("*** Data Structure element %d\n",
             count+1);
      printf("Number: %d\n", thisdata[count].numb);
      printf("Amount: %f\n", thisdata[count].amount);
```

(continues)

Listing 10.2   Continued

```
        printf("Name: %s\n\n", thisdata[count].name);
    }

    return 0;
}
```

Listing 10.2 declares an array of structures. The program then uses a for loop to query the user to enter information for each array element. After all the information has been entered, the program executes another loop, thus printing the information to the display.

Using Structures with Functions

In the same way that a regular data type can be passed to a function, a structure variable can be passed as a parameter to a function. An example is listing 10.3, which uses structures passed between functions. Examine and run listing 10.3 now.

Listing 10.3   Passing a Structure to a Function

```
/***************************************************
   STRUCTF.C - Passing a structure to a function.
***************************************************/

#include <stdio.h>

/* Structure declaration  */
struct aperson
{
   char name[25];
   int age;
};

/* Function declarations  */
struct aperson getdata(void);
void printdata(struct aperson);

int main()
{
   struct aperson friend, sister;

   printf("Please enter information about friend\n");
   friend = getdata();

   printf("Please enter information about sister\n");
   sister = getdata();

   printf("\n\n");
   printf("Friend is\n");
   printdata(friend);
```

```
    printf("Sister is\n");
    printdata(sister);

    return 0;
}
/*************************/
struct aperson getdata()
{
    struct aperson temp;
              /* Temporary, local variable */

    printf("Enter first name: ");
    scanf("%s", &temp.name);

    printf("Enter age: ");
    scanf("%d", &temp.age);

    return temp;
}

/*************************/
void printdata(struct aperson temp)
{
    printf("Name is %s \n", temp.name);
    printf("Age is %d \n\n", temp.age);
}
```

When you run the program, the output looks something like this:

```
Please enter information about friend
Enter first name: Dave
Enter age: 34
Please enter information about sister
Enter first name: Amy
Enter age: 22


Friend is
Name is Dave
Age is 34

Sister is
Name is Amy
Age is 22
```

Listing 10.3 includes two functions. One function gets information about a person (or thing) and stores it in a structure; the other function displays the contents of the structure on-screen.

Because both functions and the main program have to know how the structure is declared, this information is placed at the beginning of the program, outside the braces of both functions. This way, each function can access the information.

The function `getdata()` is called from the main program to accept information from the user. The function is declared to be type

```
struct aperson getdata()
```

because it returns a value of this type. The function also creates a temporary variable, which it uses to return to the main program.

Function `printdata()` outputs structure information to the screen. Notice that the parameters of the function are type `struct aperson`; the compiler uses this type when displaying output on-screen.

You should be beginning to see how structures provide greater flexibility and make programming easier, too. Next, you study a data structure that is similar to a structure but that provides the capability to declare variables in special situations.

Data Unions

Data unions are similar to structures in that they contain elements with data types that differ from one another. The members of a union, however, share the same area in memory. In a structure, each data element is assigned a unique memory address, but in a union, only one data member is used at any time.

In a union, the C compiler manages the memory required to store members of the data elements. It is the user's responsibility to keep track of the type of information stored at a specific time. Make sure that you are accessing the relevant data element at the right time; any attempt to access the wrong type of information produces meaningless results.

A union is allocated enough memory to hold the largest member in the declaration. If a smaller data member is active, the remaining memory is not used.

Declaring Data Unions

In general, you declare a union as follows:

```
union name
{
    datatype element1;
    datatype element2;
        .
        .
        .
    datatype elementX;
};
```

union is a reserved keyword. The other terms have the same meaning as they do in a structure declaration. Individual data items can be declared as follows:

```
union name thisname;
```

The declaration may be combined, as with structures. Thus, you can use code similar to this:

```
union name
{
    datatype element1;
    datatype element2;
       .
       .
       .
    datatype elementX;
} thisname;
```

A union can be a member of a structure, and a structure can be a member of a union. Also, structures and unions can be freely mixed with arrays. Following is an example of a union:

```
union id
{
    char name[15];
    int controlnumber;
};

union id salesitem;
```

Here, one union variable is declared: salesitem. The variable represents either a 15-character string (name) or an integer number (controlnumber) at any given time. The 15-character string requires more storage area in the computer's memory than the integer value does. Therefore, a block of memory large enough for the 15-character array is allocated to each union variable.

Enumerations

Another data type in C is data enumeration. An *enumeration* is a set of named integer constants that specifies the values that a variable of a specific type might have. The enumeration declaration enables you to assign identifiers to integer values.

Declaring Data Enumerations

Enumerations are defined much like structures, with the keyword enum used to specify the start of an enumerated type. The general format is

```
enum name { enumerationlist... } variablename;
```

The variable name is optional and can be declared separately. The name is used to declare variables of a specific type.

Following is an example of an enumerated type:

```
enum weekdays { Sun, Mon, Tue, Wed, Thu, Fri, Sat };
int day;

for (day = Sun; day <= Sat; day++)
{
    printf("The day is %d\n", day);
}
```

The first line of this code fragment uses the enum statement to assign an integer value to the name of each weekday. After the enumeration statement, whenever the name of a weekday is used, that name is replaced by the integer value assigned to it in the enumeration expression.

Following is the output of the preceding code fragment:

```
The day is 0
The day is 1
The day is 2
The day is 3
The day is 4
The day is 5
The day is 6
```

Notice that although you can refer to each day with a constant, the printf() function still displays an integer value rather than the constant. Therefore, enumerations usually are not used when frequent output to the screen is necessary.

By default, enumerations are assigned values that start with 0 and increase by increments of one to the maximum number of constants defined in the enumeration.

As you have seen, the key concept of an enumeration is that each symbol stands for an integer value. As such, these symbols can be used anywhere that an integer value normally would be used. You can specify the value of one or more of the symbols by using an *initializer*. You do this by following the symbol with an equal sign and a new integer value. For example:

```
enum weekdays { Sun, Mon=10, Tue=15,
                Wed=20, Thu=25, Fri, Sat};
```

Now the values of these symbols are as follows:

```
Sun   0
Mon   10
Tue   15
Wed   20
Thu   25
Fri   26
Sat   27
```

As you can see, whenever an initializer is used, symbols that appear after it are assigned values greater than the preceding initialization value. Listing 10.4 shows a full example of enumerated types.

Listing 10.4   Using Enumerated Types

```
/**************************************************
   ENUM.C - Using an enumerated type.
 **************************************************/

#include <stdio.h>

enum coins { penny=1, nickel=5,
             dime=10, quarter=25,
             halfdollar=50, dollar=100 };


int main()
{
    enum coins pocketchange;

    pocketchange = penny + nickel + quarter;

    printf("A penny is equal to %d\n", penny);
    printf("A nickel is equal to %d\n", nickel);
    printf("A dime is equal to %d\n", dime);
    printf("A quarter is equal to %d\n", quarter);
    printf("A half dollar is equal to %d\n", halfdollar);
    printf("A dollar is equal to %d\n", dollar);

    printf("\nThe change in my pocket is "
        "equal to %d\n", pocketchange);

    return 0;
}
```

Following is the output of the preceding program:

```
A penny is equal to 1
A nickel is equal to 5
```

```
A dime is equal to 10
A quarter is equal to 25
A half dollar is equal to 50
A dollar is equal to 100

The change in my pocket is equal to 31
```

Listing 10.4 shows you how to specify different values for each constant in the enumerated type.

User-Defined Types

The C programming language enables you to create a new name for an existing data type. This process can make program code easier to read. To create your own data names, you use the typedef statement.

Declaring User-Defined Types

Following is the general format of the typedef statement:

```
typedef type newname;
```

type is any regular data type, and *newname* is the new name of this type. The new name that you define is in addition to the existing type name.

Now look at how the typedef statement works. Suppose that you want to create a Boolean data type—that is, a variable type that is either true or false. You first declare the true and false identifier, as follows:

```
#define TRUE  1
 #define FALSE 0
```

In C, you would use an integer value for a Boolean variable. (Pascal has its own Boolean type.) Therefore, you can inform the compiler that you want to create a new data type called Boolean, which is the same as an integer. To do this, you simply precede the definition with the keyword typedef:

```
typedef int BOOL;
```

From then on, you can use BOOL to define variables, like this:

```
BOOL status;
int number;
char ch;
```

The scope of the definition depends on the location of the typedef statement. If the definition is inside a function, the scope is local. If the definition is outside the function, the scope is global.

As in the example, uppercase letters are used for the new types, to remind the user that the type name really is equivalent to another data type.

Structures and *typedef*

You can use the typedef statement in a structure so that the word struct does not have to be repeated everywhere you declare a variable of the specified structure type.

For example, you can use the following statement

```
typedef struct tagPOINT
{
    int x;
    int y;
} POINT;
```

to declare a structure that stores the *x* and *y* coordinates of a single point. Now, to declare an instance of the variable, you can use

```
POINT thispoint;
```

This saves you from having to type the keyword struct, as previously was required:

```
struct POINT thispoint;
```

By using the typedef statement, you improve the readability of your program and save time writing the program, because there is less code to type.

Manipulating Strings

Chapter 7, "Modular Programming with Functions," touched on the fact that C does not have a specific string variable type. Strings actually are character arrays. Therefore, C's operators do not allow for one string to be assigned to another. A group of functions is included in the standard C library that enables you to manipulate strings, as listed in table 10.1.

Table 10.1   String-Manipulation Functions

Function	Description
strlen()	Returns the length of a string
strchr()	Finds the first occurrence of a character
strcmp()	Compares two strings
strcat()	Appends one string to another
strcpy()	Copies one string to another

> **Note**
>
> To use any of the string-manipulation functions in your program, remember to include the STRING.H header file. STRING.H should be included at the top of your program to provide the necessary function prototypes.

The next section examines these string-manipulation functions.

The *strlen()* Function

The strlen() function returns the length of a string. Listing 10.5 shows how the function is used.

Using the *strlen()* Function

The strlen() function returns the length of a string from the beginning position to the terminating '\0' value. The general format is as follows:

    size = strlen(*string*);

string is the character array whose length you want to determine, and *size* is the resulting length of the string. For example:

```
#include <strings.h>
int x;
char str[45] = "Jack be nimble";
x = strlen(str);
```

After this code executes, x equals the integer value 14.

Listing 10.5   Finding the Length of a String

```
/***************************************************
  STR1.C - Retrieving a string length.
***************************************************/

#include <stdio.h>
#include <string.h>

int main()
{
   char str1[] = "This is a test";

   printf("<%s> \n is %d characters long",
       str1, strlen(str1) );

   return 0;
}
```

The output of the program looks like this:

```
<This is a test>
 is 14 characters long
```

The `strlen()` function returns the number of bytes that the string consumes, not counting the null-terminating character.

The *strchr()* Function

You use the `strchr()` function to find the first occurrence of a particular character in a specified string. The terminating null character is included in the search; therefore, you also can search for the null character in a string.

If the specified character is found, the function returns a pointer to the first occurrence of the character in the string.

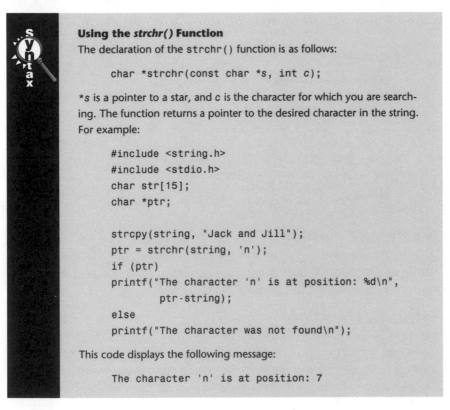

Using the *strchr()* Function

The declaration of the `strchr()` function is as follows:

```
char *strchr(const char *s, int c);
```

s is a pointer to a star, and *c* is the character for which you are searching. The function returns a pointer to the desired character in the string. For example:

```
#include <string.h>
#include <stdio.h>
char str[15];
char *ptr;

strcpy(string, "Jack and Jill");
ptr = strchr(string, 'n');
if (ptr)
printf("The character 'n' is at position: %d\n",
        ptr-string);
else
printf("The character was not found\n");
```

This code displays the following message:

```
The character 'n' is at position: 7
```

Listing 10.6 shows you how to use the `strchr()` function.

Listing 10.6   Using the *strchr( )* Function

```
/**************************************************
   STR2.C - Finding a character in a string.
 **************************************************/

#include <stdio.h>
#include <string.h>


int main()
{
    char str[80], ch;
    char *location;

    puts("Enter a string: ");
    gets(str);

    puts("Enter search character: ");
    ch = getchar();

    location = strchr(str, ch);

    if (location == NULL)
    {
        puts("\nCharacter not in buffer");
    }
    else
    {
        printf("\nString is %s", location);
    }

    return 0;
}
```

The *strcmp( )* Function

To compare two strings, use the strcmp() function. Because a C program
cannot use operators to compare strings (as a BASIC program can), a built-in
function is provided for this purpose.

The *strcat( )* Function

Use the strcat() function to append (or concatenate) one string to another.
The strcat() function is passed two strings as parameters. The function ap-
pends the second string to the first one, terminating the resulting string with
a null character. Listing 10.7 shows you how to use the strcat() function.

Using the *strcmp()* Function

The general format of the strcmp() function is

```
int strcmp(const char *s1, const char*s2);
```

The function takes two parameters—the two strings you are comparing. The parameters are represented in the code as *s1* and *s2*. The function returns a true value if the strings are equal; otherwise, the value is false. For example, you could use this statement:

```
strcmp("P", "P");
```

The preceding statement returns a true value. The following statement returns a false value, because the two strings are not equivalent:

```
strcmp("A", "B");
```

Remember that the strcmp() function is case-sensitive—that is, if you pass the function two strings with mixed case, it will return a false value even if the strings are the same.

Using the *strcat()* Function

The declaration for the strcat() function appears like this:

```
char *strcat(char *test, const char *src);
```

src is a pointer to the first string, and *test* is the destination string. The function returns a pointer to the combined string. For example:

```
char destination[25];
char *space = " ", *one = "One", *two = "Two";

strcpy(destination, two);
strcat(destination, space);
strcat(destination, one);

printf("%s\n", destination);
```

This code outputs a string that reads as follows:

```
One Two
```

> ### Caution
>
> You must allocate enough space for the resulting string. If, after the second string is appended to the first string, the resulting string exceeds the allocated size of the first string, the strcat() function might destroy other data and cause memory corruption. See listing 10.7 for an example of the strcat() function.

Listing 10.7   Using the *strcat()* Function

```
/**************************************************
   STR3.C - Using the strcat() function.
 **************************************************/

#include <stdio.h>
#include <string.h>

int main()
{
   char fullname[50];
   char middle[15];
   char lastname[15];

   puts("Type your first name: ");
   gets(fullname);

   puts("Type your middle name: ");
   gets(middle);

   puts("Type your last name: ");
   gets(lastname);

   strcat(fullname, " ");
   strcat(fullname, middle);
   strcat(fullname, " ");
   strcat(fullname, lastname);

   printf("\nHello %s\n", fullname);

   return 0;
}
```

The output of the program looks like this:

```
Type your first name:
George
Type your middle name:
Thomas
Type your last name:
Washington

Hello George Thomas Washington
```

The strcat() function combines the three strings. Notice that in between combining the strings, the program inserts the space character. This might be necessary in your program, depending on the type of processing you are doing.

The *strcpy()* Function

To copy one string to another, use the strcpy() function. The function takes two parameters and copies the second string to the first string. The terminating null character of the second string also is copied, so the first string becomes an exact copy of the second string.

Using the *strcpy()* Function

The format of the strcpy() function is

```
char *strcpy(char *test, const char *src);
```

src is a pointer to the source string, and *test* is a pointer to the destination string. The function returns a pointer to the copied string. For example:

```
char str1[60] = "Copying strings is easy";
char, str2[60];


strcpy(str2, str1);

printf("%s", str1);
```

The output of the program displays the string "Copying strings is easy".

Other String Functions

Most compilers provide other functions for manipulating strings. There are many different functions for performing different string manipulations. Borland C, for example, has functions that convert a string to uppercase, convert a string to lowercase, and reverse strings. Check your compiler's manual for the extended functions that your compiler provides.

Summary

This chapter examined some of the more advanced data structures in the C programming language. You learned about data structures, unions, data enumerations, type definitions, and functions for manipulating strings. The chapter covered the following important points:

■ *Structures* enable you to combine unrelated types of data in a single variable. When you use a structure, you first must declare the structure and then define the structure as a variable, which allocates the memory for the structure.

■ Structure elements are accessed by referring to the base name of the structure, separated by a period, followed by the name of the element that you want to access.

■ *Arrays of structures* enable you to access structure elements in a loop by using the same base name for each array element in the structure.

■ Like structures, *data unions* contain several different elements; however, the data items inside a union share the given memory location. The union takes the size of the largest data member.

■ An *enumeration* is a set of named integer constants that specifies the values that a variable of a specific type can have. The enumeration declaration enables you to assign identifiers to integer values.

■ The C programming language enables you to create a new name for an existing data type. This feature can make program code easier to read. To create your own data names, use the `typedef` statement.

■ Because the C programming language does not explicitly have a string variable type, functions are provided for manipulating strings. The functions discussed in this chapter are `strlen()`, `strchr()`, `strcmp()`, `strcat()`, and `strcpy()`.

Chapter 11

Working with Files

Disk files are essential to computers. File access is used in every type of application (word processing, spreadsheet, and database), as well as many other types of utilities. Files are used to store programs, documents, data, and information of all kinds. As a programmer, you have to write programs that create files, write data into files, and read data from files.

There are two types of file access: *sequential access* and *random access*. Sequential-file access refers to the fact that a program must read the contents at the beginning of a file before it can read data at the end of the file.

Sequential access is analogous to the way an audio cassette tape operates. With a cassette tape, you must go through the songs at the beginning of the tape (either by playing them or fast-forwarding through them) before reaching the songs at the end of the tape.

Random-file access, on the other hand, enables you to find a specific location in the file without having to read through the preceding data. Random-access file I/O (input/output) is analogous to the way a compact disc player (or a record player) operates. You can select any song on the disc (or record) without having to go through the preceding selections.

In this chapter, you learn how to process files using standard C input and output functions. You learn about I/O modes, character I/O, string I/O, and formatted I/O functions.

The File Pointer

The FILE data type is commonly referred to as the *file pointer*. It is actually a pointer to the information that defines various characteristics about the file—including its file name, status, and current offset position. The file pointer identifies a specific disk file. The file pointer is used by the stream associated with it to direct the operation of the input and output functions.

The file pointer is a structure defined in the STDIO.H include file. It is not important to know exactly for what every element of the FILE structure is used, but you can examine the STDIO.H header file for the structure definition. Most of the information is internal to the compiler, so it's not directly useful to the programmer.

Declaring a File Pointer

To obtain a file-pointer variable in your own programs, declare one in a manner similar to this:

```
FILE *fptr;
```

in which *fptr* is the name of the file pointer. It can be any name up to 32 characters long; however, the length is usually six to ten characters long.

You can now make use of the file I/O functions, which require a file pointer as one of their parameters. The following line declares a file pointer with the name inputfile.

```
FILE *inputfile;
```

Later, this file pointer is used with the file I/O routines to access disk files.

Opening a File

Before you can read or write to a disk file, you must first open the file. Opening a file establishes an understanding between the program and DOS regarding which file is to be accessed and how it is to be accessed. The fopen() function is used for this purpose. It takes two parameters and returns a variable of type FILE.

Using the *fopen( )* Function

The fopen() function is declared as follows:

```
FILE *fopen(const char filename, const char "mode");
```

in which *filename* is a string of characters that comprise a file name. The *filename* can include a path specification. The *mode* parameter determines how the file is opened—it is a string, and therefore is always surrounded by double quotation marks. Acceptable values for the *mode* parameter are listed in table 11.1.

As mentioned earlier, the fopen() function returns a file pointer. If an error occurs when you try to open the file, the fopen() function returns

a NULL pointer. The following statement opens the CONFIG.SYS file in read mode:

```
FILE *fileptr;
fileptr = fopen("CONFIG.SYS", "r");
```

Table 11.1   Acceptable File-Mode Indicators

String	Meaning
r	Open file for reading only. File must already exist.
w	Create file for writing. If a file by that name already exists, it is overwritten.
a	Append, open for writing at end of file, or create for writing if the file does not exist.
r+	Open an existing file for update (reading and writing).
w+	Create a new file for update (reading and writing). If a file by that name already exists, it is overwritten.
a+	Open for append, open for update at the end of the file, or create if the file does not exist.

Note

Your program should not alter the values in the FILE structure directly because they are manipulated by the file input and output routines. Therefore, if you try to change one manually, the values in the structure don't correspond to the expectations of the routines.

If you wanted to open a file to retrieve information, you would use a statement similar to this one:

```
FILE *fptr;
fptr = fopen("C:\\TEST.DAT", "w");
```

However, you probably also want to test the return value to ensure that the file was opened correctly. To do this, you use the following code segment:

```
FILE *fptr;
if ((fileptr = fopen("C:\\TEST.DAT", "r")) == NULL)
{
    printf("Error: Cannot open input file\n");
    exit(0);
}
```

Using this method, you detect any errors that might have occurred while opening the file.

> **Note**
>
> When specifying your file name on DOS machines, you can specify the full path of the file along with its name. However, because C uses the backslash character as a control character in a string, you must use two backslashes (\ \) to inform the compiler that you want to use the actual backslash character.

Using Character File I/O

Once you have opened a file, you are ready to write data to it or read data from it. Probably the simplest way this can be done is with the fgetc() and fputc() functions. They work very much like the functions getchar() and putchar(). The difference is that you must tell them which file to use. You specify the file by passing the file pointer received from the fopen() function.

Reading Characters

Listing 11.1 is a program that mimics the MS-DOS TYPE command. It is called TYPER.C and its purpose is to prompt you for a file (it is a bit friendlier than TYPE), then display the contents of the file on-screen.

If the amount of characters in the file is longer than what can be displayed in a single screen, the text is scrolled off the top of the screen—enabling you to view the entire file. The program works best when you view an ASCII file because you are able to understand the information contained in the file.

Listing 11.1   The TYPER.C Program

```
/***************************************************
   TYPER.C - Sends character read from the file
             to the display.
   ***************************************************/

#include <stdio.h>
#include <stdlib.h>

int main()
{
   char ch, filename[85];
   FILE *fileptr;

   printf("\nPlease Enter filename: ");
   gets(filename);

   if ((fileptr = fopen(filename, "r")) == NULL)
   {
```

```
        printf("Error: Cannot open input file\n");
        exit(0);
    }

    printf("\n\n***Listing of: %s***\n", filename);

    while (!feof(fileptr))
    {
        ch = fgetc(fileptr);
                        /* Get next character from file */
        putchar(ch); /* Display character on-screen  */
    }

    fclose(fileptr);

    return 0;
}
```

The logic behind the program is rather simple. It starts by getting the file name to display from the user. It then tries to open the file. If there is an error, the user is notified and the program aborts.

If there is no error, the program enters a while loop. It gets the next character from the file with the fgetc() function, and displays that character on-screen with the putchar() function.

Notice a few new concepts in this program. First, the while loop uses the return value from a function called feof(), as follows:

```
    while (!feof(fileptr))
    {
        ch = fgetc(fileptr);
                        /* Get next character from file */
        putchar(ch);  /* Display character on-screen */
    }
```

The feof() function checks for the end-of-file (EOF) marker. The end-of-file marker is a special character that operating systems place at the end of each file instructing the system that the file is at its end. Therefore, in this program you can continue reading characters until reaching the end-of-file marker. When the feof() function is true, you exit the while loop and close the file.

The last function call in the program is fclose(). The fclose() function closes the file identified by the file pointer's parameter. The function returns a value identifying whether it was able to close the file. This simple program did not check for the value. In most cases, you do not have problems closing your files.

Writing Characters

The function that writes a single character to the file is putc(). It is the complement to the fgetc() function.

Using the *putc( )* Function

The general form of the putc() function is

```
int putc(int c, FILE fileptr);
```

The value, *c,* is an integer value that specifies what value should be written to the file. The *fileptr* points to a previously defined FILE variable that has been opened. The following code writes a single character to a file named FILE.TXT:

```
FILE *fptr;
fptr = fopen("FILE.TXT", "w");
putc("P", fptr);
fclose(fptr);
```

Listing 11.2 writes characters to a file.

Listing 11.2 This Program Writes Characters to a File

```
/**************************************************
   WRITER.C - Sends characters to a text file.
 **************************************************/

#include <stdio.h>
#include <stdlib.h>
#include <process.h>

int main()
{
   char ch, filename[85];
   FILE *fileptr;

   printf("\nEnter filename: ");
   gets(filename);

   printf("\n\nType # on a blank line to end\n\n");

   if ((fileptr = fopen(filename, "w")) == NULL)
   {
      printf("Error: Cannot open input file\n");
      exit(0);
   }
```

```
        while ((ch=getchar()) != '#')
        {
           putc(ch, fileptr);
        }
        fclose(fileptr);

        return 0;
    }
```

This program sits in a loop and records every character you type in the file until you type # on a blank line and press Enter. At that point, the file closes and the program ends. Notice that the `fclose()` function writes all data in the file I/O buffers to disk.

Notice that your disk is not accessed each time you type a character. The keystrokes you type are stored into a buffer. The buffer is not written to disk until it fills up or until you use the `fclose()` function to close the file.

> **Caution**
>
> If you neglect to call the `fclose()` function when writing data to a file, you may lose some of your data.

You can experiment with the previous two programs by using WRITER.C to create an ASCII text file, then using TYPER.C to display the contents of the file.

Using String I/O Functions

It probably seems like an awful hassle having to read characters in from a file, one at a time. Luckily, the C library has functions that read or write an entire line of text at a time. Reading and writing strings of characters from and to files is about as easy as reading and writing individual characters.

The `fputs()` function writes a string of characters and the `fgets()` function reads a string of characters. Think of these functions as the file versions of the `puts()` and `gets()` functions.

Reading Strings

Listing 11.3 is similar to the earlier TYPER.C program. However, it reads a line of text in from a file (rather than single characters) and displays them on-screen. It also keeps track of how many lines it has read and informs the user how many lines of text are in the file.

Listing 11.3 STRREAD.C Reads a File as a Text String

```c
/*****************************************
   STRREAD.C - Reads strings from disk.
*****************************************/

#include <stdio.h>
#include <stdio.h>
#include <process.h>
#define MAXLINELEN 135

int main()
{
   char filename[85], strline[MAXLINELEN];
   int line = 0;
   FILE *fileptr;

   printf("\nEnter filename: ");
   gets(filename);

   if ((fileptr = fopen(filename, "r")) == NULL)
   {
      printf("Error: Cannot open input file\n");
      exit(0);
   }

   while (!feof(fileptr))
   {
      fgets(strline, MAXLINELEN, fileptr);
      printf("%s",strline);
      line++;
   }
   fclose(fileptr);

   printf("\n***There were %d lines "
          "in that file\n", line);

   return 0;
}
```

> **Note**
>
> This program used a maximum input length of 135 characters. However, you can use any string length that you need in your own programs.

The new function in this program is fgets(). It is used in the following context.

The *fgets( )* Function

The syntax for the fgets() function takes the following form:

fgets(*strline*, *MAXLINELEN*, *fileptr*);

The fgets() function takes three parameters. The first is the character array where the string is to be stored (*strline*). The second is the maximum length of characters read into the string (*MAXLINELEN*). This second parameter prevents the fgets() function from reading too long of a string and accessing beyond the bounds of the array. The third parameter is the file pointer (*fileptr*), which informs the function which file to access.

Writing Strings

Just as easily as you were able to write characters, you can write an entire string at once. Listing 11.4 shows a program that prompts for some strings and then writes them to a file.

Listing 11.4   STRWRITE.C, a Program that Writes Strings to a Disk File

```
/**********************************************
   STRWRITE.C - Write strings to disk file.
**********************************************/

#include <stdio.h>
#include <stdlib.h>
#include <string.h>

#define MAXLINELEN 135

int main()
{
   char filename[85], strline[MAXLINELEN];
   FILE *fileptr;

   printf("\nPress Enter on a blank line to exit.");

   printf("\nEnter filename to write to: ");
   gets(filename);

   if ((fileptr = fopen(filename, "w")) == NULL)
   {
      printf("Error: Cannot open input file\n");
      exit(0);
   }

   while (strlen(gets(strline)) > 0 )
   {
      fputs(strline, fileptr);
      fputs("\n", fileptr);
```

(continues)

Listing 11.4 Continued

```
    }

    fclose(fileptr);

    return 0;
}
```

The user is first prompted for a file name to which to write the text. The user then types a series of lines. Each line is terminated by pressing the Enter key. To exit the program, the user presses the Enter key as the first character in the line. The program then writes the file to disk.

The main loop of the program checks the length of the string (using the strlen() function). If the length of the string is 0 (which means the user pressed Enter on the first line), the loop aborts. Otherwise, the fputs() function outputs the string to the open file.

The fputs() function does not automatically output a carriage return—you use a second fputs("\n") line to output a carriage return to the file.

Formatted Input/Output

So far, you have looked solely at getting or writing ASCII text. First, you looked at character I/O, then string I/O. However, the designers of C were smart enough to know that there are other types of data that you might want to write or read in a file.

That obvious choice of data is numerical data. In C, this is called formatted file input and output. It enables you to handle numerical (and string) data very nicely. With formatted input and output, you treat a file as if you were prompting or writing output, similar to using printf() and scanf().

These functions work almost exactly like printf() and scanf(), except they operate with disk files and take a FILE pointer as their first parameter. By now, you might be able to guess what the names of the functions are (most of the functions that operate on files are prefixed with the character *f*).

Using the Formatted Input/Output Functions

The formatted input/output functions work almost identically to the ones you already know. They each take an additional parameter, which is that of the file pointer. The functions are declared as follows:

```
int fprintf (FILE *stream,
                const char *format [, argument, ...]);
```

and

```
int fscanf (FILE *stream,
                const char *format [, address, ...]);
```

Basically, you specify a file pointer and the C functions do all the work. The functions use the same format specifiers you have used. They are similar to the `printf()` and `scanf()` functions, except they use disk files. The following example shows how to send output to the current file using the `fprintf()` function:

```
fprintf(fptr, "The value of "
                "the variable is %d", 1+5+17);
```

Next is an example of the `fscanf()` function. It gets the value of an integer value from the file and stores it in the variable x, as follows:

```
fscanf(fptr, "%d", x)
```

The *fprintf( )* Function

Listing 11.5 is an example of formatted I/O using the `fprintf()` function. It creates a data file with two pieces of information for each record—a person's name and age.

Listing 11.5   FORMIO.C Sample Program

```
/***************************************
  FORMIO.C - Uses formatted file output.
 ***************************************/

#include <stdio.h>
#include <process.h>
#include <conio.h>
#include <string.h>
#include <ctype.h>

int main()
{
   char cont[2];
   char name[25];
   int age;
   FILE *fileptr;
```

(continues)

Listing 11.5   Continued

```
if ((fileptr = fopen("NAMES.DAT", "w")) == NULL)
{
   printf("Error: Cannot open input file\n");
   exit(0);
}

strcpy(cont, "Y");

while ( strcmp("Y", cont) == 0)
{
   printf("Enter Name: \n");
   scanf("%s", name);
   printf("Enter Age: \n");
   scanf("%i", &age);
   fprintf(fileptr, "%s %d\n", name, age);
   printf("Do you want to enter another"
      "name? (Y/N)");
   scanf("%s", cont);
   cont[0] = toupper(cont[0]);
}

fclose(fileptr);

return 0;
}
```

The program creates a data file that is similar to one that would be used in a database. The program creates a loop that continuously asks for more information to write to the disk. Each time the program is about to restart the loop, it asks if you want to write another piece of information.

The core of the program is the `fprintf()` function. It takes one more parameter than the normal `printf()` function (the one you have used since Chapter 1). The extra parameter is the file pointer. That pointer refers to the file to which you want to write. The `fprintf()` function takes the same format specifiers as the `printf()` statement; therefore, it provides an easy way to write a lot of different information to a file.

The *fscanf( )* Function

Once you have written out formatted data, you have to read it into your program. The `fscanf()` function does just that—it reads the specified data from a file into your program.

Listing 11.6 demonstrates how this can be done. Listing 11.7 is an example of a data file you might use with the program.

Listing 11.6   FORMAT2.C Program

```c
/*******************************************
  FORMAT2.C - Uses formatted file input.
*******************************************/

#include <stdio.h>
#include <process.h>
#include <stdlib.h>


int main()
{
   char buffer[25];
   int number;
   FILE *fileptr;

   if ((fileptr = fopen("NAMES.DAT", "r")) == NULL)
   {
      printf("Error: Cannot open input file\n");
      exit(0);
   }

   while (!feof(fileptr))
   {
      fscanf(fileptr, "%s", buffer);
      printf("Name = %s, ", buffer);

      fscanf(fileptr, "%d", &number);
      printf("Age = %d\n", number);
   }

   fclose(fileptr);

   return 0;

}
```

Listing 11.7   Example NAMES.DAT Data File

```
Mike 24
Matt 34
Lori 55
Gary 12
Jenny 27
```

The program loops until the end-of-file marker is detected. The `fscanf()` function reads in the data. It takes an extra parameter, which identifies the `FILE` pointer.

It is important to realize that the formatted I/O functions create data files that are regular ASCII files. The data is not stored in any cryptic notation. This makes it easier to re-create the files if they become damaged. You can use a regular text editor to enter the data manually.

Random-Access File I/O

Random-access file input and output enables you to access any part of a file without having to first read in earlier parts of the file. You can treat the file like an array and move directly to any particular byte in the file.

> **Note**
>
> Remember that random-access file I/O is similar to finding songs on an audio compact disc (or record player). That is, you can easily skip to any song on the compact disc. You don't have to listen to the first song before you can listen to the second song. Similarly, random-access file I/O enables you to go to any point in the file and start reading data in (or writing data out).

When working with random-access file I/O, a program uses the same `fopen()` and `fclose()` functions as with sequential I/O. You can still use the sequential file I/O functions to get data, once you have told the system where in the file to go.

Although random-access file I/O is similar to sequential I/O, there are differences as well. One of the biggest differences is that when files are opened for random-access I/O, they are usually opened in binary format. This means that the data file that results is not an ASCII text file and cannot be easily re-created with a text editor.

Storing data in binary format is quicker for the computer. It also makes it easier for C routines to read and write the data. Another important point about storing data in binary format is that it requires less disk space to store.

Suppose, for example, you want to store the number 20 to disk. If you store the number using text format, that number requires two bytes (one byte for the 2 and another byte for the 0). However, if you store that number in binary format, it only requires one byte—a storage reduction of 50 percent! In large applications, this amount can be significant.

To see how random-access file I/O works, type the following program (listing 11.8) and run it. It prompts you for an ASCII text file, and then displays a file in reverse order.

Listing 11.8   Displays a File in Reverse Order

```
/***************************************************
   BACK.C - Displays file backward with
            random-access file input.
 ***************************************************/

#include <stdio.h>
#include <process.h>
```

```c
int main()
{
   char ch, filename[85];
   FILE *fileptr;
   long lastpos;

   printf("\nEnter filename: ");
   gets(filename);

   if ((fileptr = fopen(filename, "r")) == NULL)
   {
      printf("Error: Cannot open input file\n");
      exit(0);
   }

   fseek(fileptr, 0, SEEK_END);
   lastpos = ftell(fileptr);

   while ( !feof(fileptr) )
   {
      fseek(fileptr, --lastpos, SEEK_SET);
      ch = fgetc(fileptr);
      putchar(ch);
   }

   fclose(fileptr);

   return 0;
}
```

Here is a sample file called QUOTES.DAT. Sample output from the program with this file looks like this:

```
Enter filename: c:\temp\quotes.dat
?eerga uoy t'noD
egaugnal etirovaf ym si C_
```

You can use this program on any ASCII data file. Most of this program's statements should look familiar to you. However, there are two new functions you need to examine: fseek() and ftell().

Using the *fseek ( )* Function

The fseek() function enables you to move to any location in a file. The function takes three parameters, and is declared as follows:

```
int fseek(FILE *stream, long offset, int whence);
```

The first of the three arguments is a FILE pointer to the file being accessed. The file pointer is returned from a call to the fopen() function.

The second argument, offset, is of type long and is an offset in the file. This parameter instructs you how far to move from the starting point.

(continues)

(continued)

The offset can be positive, in which case you move forward, or the offset can be negative, in which case you move backward. If the offset is 0, you don't move the file location.

The third argument is called whence, and it identifies the starting point from which the offset is calculated. The STDIO.H header file specifies the constants in table 11.2, which can be used for the whence parameter.

The fseek() function returns 0 if successful. It returns a nonzero value if there was an error in moving to a specific location.

Table 11.2 STDIO.H's Constants Used for the *whence* Parameter

Constant Name	Value	Measure Offset From
SEEK_SET	0	Beginning of file
SEEK_CUR	1	Current position
SEEK_END	2	End of file

The ftell() function returns a long data type describing the current file position. It actually returns the number of bytes from the beginning of the file. The first byte is numbered byte 0.

In listing 11.8, you first use the fseek() function to move to the end of the file (you use the SEEK_END constant). You then use the ftell() function to return the current file location. That location is stored in the variable, lastpos.

From that point, you set up a while loop, which follows:

```
while ( !feof(fileptr) )
{
    fseek(fileptr, --lastpos, SEEK_SET);
    ch = fgetc(fileptr);
    putchar(ch);
}
```

This loop moves backward from the last byte in the file by decrementing the lastpos variable. It then reads in the character at the specified location (using the fgetc() function) and displays it on-screen with the putchar() function.

Interestingly enough, when you are reading in reverse mode like this, you can still use the feof() function to check for the beginning of the file.

When all the characters in the file have been read, the loop is exited and the `fclose()` function is called to close the file.

At this point, you may be thinking to yourself that random-access file I/O sounds somewhat useful. However, you might not see the practical uses of random-access file I/O. After all, although it might be nice to read a file in backward, it is not one of the most common features of most word processors.

In order to understand how useful random-access file I/O is, you must learn about a few other reading and writing functions. Thus, you next learn how to read and write entire data structures out to disk, all at one time.

Writing Structures

Remember that structures are groups of uncommon data types. The following example program (listing 11.9) uses a simple structure with two data elements. The program continues to ask the user to enter records. When the user is done entering data, the program stores the data in a disk file.

Listing 11.9   Writing Data Structures to Disk

```
/**************************************************
   STRUCTW.C - Writes structure data to disk.
 **************************************************/

#include <stdio.h>
#include <string.h>
#include <process.h>
#include <ctype.h>

struct inforec
{
   char name[85];
   int age;
};

int main()
{
   char ch = 'N';
   char filename[85];
   FILE *fileptr;
   struct inforec person;

   printf("\nEnter filename: ");
   gets(filename);

   if ((fileptr = fopen(filename, "w")) == NULL)
   {
      printf("Error: Cannot open input file\n");
      exit(0);
   }
```

(continues)

Listing 11.9   Continued

```
        do
        {
            printf("\nEnter Name: ");
            scanf("%s", person.name);

            printf("Enter Age: ");
            scanf("%d", &person.age);

            fwrite(&person, sizeof(person), 1, fileptr);

            fflush(stdin);

            printf("Care to add another name "
                    "to database? (Y/N)");
            ch = getchar();
        }
        while (toupper(ch) == 'Y');

        fclose(fileptr);
        printf("\n\nFile %s successfully "
                "saved to disk\n", filename);

        return 0;
    }
```

Here is sample interaction with the program:

```
Enter filename: c:\temp\club.dat

Enter Name: Bob
Enter Age: 33
Care to add another name to database? (Y/N)

y
Enter Name: Tim
Enter Age: 17
Care to add another name to database? (Y/N)

n

File c:\temp\club.dat successfully saved to disk
```

You can enter as many data records into the database as you have memory for (I think you would probably get bored of entering records before you run out of memory). The new function in this program is called fwrite().

Using the *fwrite( )* Function

The fwrite() function is declared as follows:

```
size_t fwrite(const void *ptr, size_t size,
              size_t n, FILE*stream);
```

The function takes four arguments. The first argument, *ptr, is a buffer location in which to store data. The second argument specifies how many bytes to write. The third argument specifies how many records to write. Finally, the last parameter is a FILE pointer, which (as you know) was returned from the fopen() function.

The fwrite() function writes out a block of data. In the previous program, you wrote out a block of memory the length of the structure (it was easy to use the sizeof() function and allow the compiler to do the byte-counting. The function returns the number of records written, not the number of bytes). Usually, the function returns 1. If it returns 0, the write operation was unsuccessful. The following code sample writes the contents of a character array to disk:

```
FILE *fptr;
char str[10];
fwrite(&str, sizeof(str), 1, fptr);
```

Now that you have this file created and on disk, you need some way of reading it back in. That is exactly what you learn next.

Reading Structures

The counterpart to the fwrite() function is the fread() function. This function reads in a specific number of bytes and stores the data in a memory location.

Using the *fread( )* Function

This is the declaration for the fread() function:

```
size_t fread(void *ptr, size_t size,
             size_t n, FILE *stream);
```

The parameters are similar to the fwrite() function. The first is the address of a buffer in which to store the data being read. The second instructs how many bytes to read in for each record. The third parameter instructs how many records to read in. The last parameter is a FILE pointer to your open file. The following code sample reads a 10-character array from a disk file:

(continues)

(continued)

```
        FILE *fptr;
        char str[10];
        fread(&str, sizeof(str), 1, fptr);
```

Listing 11.10 (STRUCTR.C) is an example program that reads a data file that was created in the previous program, STRUCTW.C.

Listing 11.10   Reads Structures from Disk

```c
/***********************************************
   STRUCTR.C -Reads structures from disk file.
 ***********************************************/

#include <stdio.h>
#include <stdlib.h>
#include <process.h>

struct inforec
{
   char name[85];
   int age;
};

int main()
{
   char ch, filename[85];
   FILE *fileptr;
   int recnumb = 1;
   struct inforec person;

   printf("\nEnter filename: ");
   gets(filename);

   if ((fileptr = fopen(filename, "r")) == NULL)
   {
      printf("Error: Cannot open input file\n");
      exit(0);
   }

   while ( fread(&person, sizeof(person),
           1, fileptr) == 1 )
   {
      printf("Record # %d\n", recnumb++);
      printf("Name is %s\n", person.name);
      printf("Age is %d\n", person.age);
      printf("Press ENTER to view next record\n\n");
      ch = getchar();
   }
```

```
        fclose(fileptr);
        printf("***End of file reached***\n");

        return 0;
}
```

Now that you are able to write data out using the `fwrite()` function and read it back in with the `fread()` function, you know exactly where on the disk the data is being saved. This is when your random-access file input and output functions really shine.

Reading and Writing Arrays

In the same way that you were able to use the `fread()` or `fwrite()` functions to read or write a data structure, you can read and write any data type, including arrays.

Listing 11.11 demonstrates how to load and save arrays. Rather than splitting functionality between two programs, this single program writes a data file, then reads it back in.

Listing 11.11   Random-Access File Operations on an Array

```
/*****************************************
   RWARRAY.C - Reads and writes an array.
 *****************************************/

#include <stdio.h>
#include <stdlib.h>
#include <process.h>

#define ITEMS 7

int main()
{
    char filename[85];
    int count;
    FILE *fileptr;
    int data[ITEMS] = {8, 57, 5, 309, 33, 87, 55 };
    int data2[ITEMS];

    printf("\nEnter filename: ");
    gets(filename);

    /* Write array into a file */
    if ((fileptr = fopen(filename, "w")) == NULL)
    {
        printf("Error: Cannot open file\n");
        exit(0);
    }

    printf("Writing data items to "
```

(continues)

Listing 11.11 Continued

```
                     "file %s...\n", filename);

        fwrite(data, sizeof(data), 1, fileptr);
        fclose(fileptr);        /* Close the file */

        /* Read file into an array */
        if ((fileptr = fopen(filename, "r")) == NULL)
        {   /*  Check return value just to make sure  */
            printf("Error: Cannot open input file\n");
            exit(0);
        }

        printf("Reading data items from file...\n");
        fread(&data2, sizeof(data), 1, fileptr);
        fclose(fileptr);

        printf("The elements of the array are \n");
        for (count=0; count < ITEMS; count++)
        {
            printf("Element %d is %d\n",
                    count, data2[count]);

        }

        return 0;
    }
```

Sample output of the program looks like this:

```
Enter filename: c:\temp\numbers.dat
Writing data items to file c:\temp\numbers.dat...
Reading data items from file...
The elements of the array are
Element 0 is 8
Element 1 is 57
Element 2 is 5
Element 3 is 309
Element 4 is 33
Element 5 is 87
Element 6 is 55
```

The program stores an array of seven elements into a user-specified disk file. It then reads them back into a separate file and displays the elements on-screen.

You could have written the data elements one at a time using formatted output (with the `fprintf()` function); however, writing the whole array out to disk with one statement is much more efficient. Not only does it take less space, it is also faster to load and save the array.

Summary

Disk file input and output is an important part of any program. In this chapter, you learned how to access files in a variety of ways, including both sequential and random-access file I/O. The following important points were covered:

- Before you can access a file, you must use the *fopen() function* to gain access to the specific file. In the call to the function, you specify the file name and the mode in which you want to access the file.

- The *fclose() function* is used to close a disk file after it has been opened.

- Every file has an *end-of-file (EOF) marker* attached at the end. Your program can use this marker to indicate when it has reached the end of the file. The feof() function returns a value that informs you if the EOF marker has been reached.

- The *FILE pointer* stores essential information about the location and offset of a data file.

- *Character-file I/O* enables you to read or write a single character of information from a disk file.

- The *string I/O functions* enable you to read or write an entire line of text from your disk files at once.

- The *formatted I/O functions* enable you to create data files that create both alphabetic characters and numeric text.

- *Random-access file input and output* enables you to access any byte of information in a file without having to read in any of the previous file contents. The process is similar to that of locating songs on an audio compact disc. You can instantly go to any location on the disk.

- By storing information in binary format, file I/O is more efficient because memory is conserved and the read and write operations are quicker.

- The two main functions that allow a program to use random-access file I/O are *fseek()* and *ftell()*. The fseek() function moves to any specific location in a file. The ftell() function returns the current location in the file.

- A specific number of bytes of data can be written to disk at once with the *fwrite() function*. This function enables you to save an entire data structure or array with a single statement. Once you write out a number of bytes to disk with the fwrite() function, you can read that data back in with the fread() function. The *fread() function* reads a specified number of bytes into a buffer.

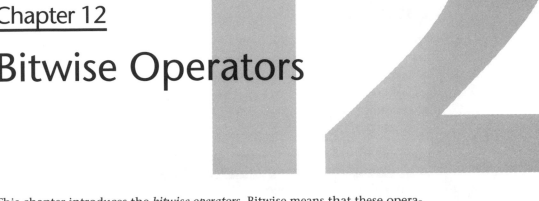

Chapter 12

Bitwise Operators

This chapter introduces the *bitwise operators*. Bitwise means that these operators operate on the bits one at a time, not on the value of the variable taken as a whole. The existence of these operators is one reason for the popularity of C among programmers who write device drivers and operating system internal code. These features allow C to behave much like an assembly language if needed. They operate on internal representations of data, not just "values in variables," as the other operators do. Bitwise operators require an understanding of the binary numbering system and of your PC's memory.

All of the data in your computer is stored as 1s and 0s. The bitwise operators allow you to update and read these bits individually. System software programmers, on the other hand, do much of their work in data structures called *control blocks*. To keep these control blocks as small as possible, these programmers pack as much information as possible into each byte of memory. They like the bitwise operators because they can store as many as 32 individual pieces of information.

Some people program in C for years and don't know the bitwise operators. Most application programmers avoid them unless they have a compelling need to employ them. Nevertheless, understanding them can help improve the efficiency of your programs and let you operate at a deeper level than many programming languages allow.

In this chapter, you learn about the following topics:

- The bitwise logical operators
- Performing bitwise operations internally
- The bitwise shift operators
- The compound bitwise operators

Bitwise Logical Operators

There are four bitwise logical operators, shown in table 12.1. Because these operators work on the binary representation of integer data, systems programmers can manipulate internal bits in memory and variables. The bitwise logical operators are not just for systems programmers, however. Application programmers can also improve portions of their programs by learning how to use these operators.

Table 12.1 The Bitwise Logical Operators	
Operator	**Meaning**
&	Bitwise AND
¦	Bitwise inclusive OR
^	Bitwise exclusive OR
~	Bitwise 1's complement

Each bitwise logical operator performs a bit-by-bit operation on internal data. Bitwise operators apply only to char, int, and long variables and constants, not to floating-point data. Because binary numbers consist of 1s and 0s, these 1s and 0s (called *bits*) are manipulated to produce the desired result of each bitwise operator.

Tables 12.2 through 12.5 are truth tables that describe the actions of the bitwise operators on the internal bit patterns of an int (or char or long).

The Bitwise & (AND)

The & operator is called the bitwise AND. It sets a bit to 1 if either of the corresponding bits is 0. If both of the bits are 0, the & sets the corresponding bit in the result to 0. You use the bitwise & (AND) to test whether both bits are set to 1. Table 12.2 shows the truth table that C uses to evaluate the & (AND) operator.

Table 12.2 The Bitwise & (AND) Truth Table			
First Bit	**AND**	**Second Bit**	**Result**
1	&	1	1
1	&	0	0
0	&	1	0
0	&	0	0

The Bitwise & (AND)

The bitwise & (AND) combines two variables in a bit-by-bit fashion. The syntax is

```
var1 = var2 & var3;
```

The result is a variable that has the bitwise ANDed combination

Example

You can test and change individual bits inside variables to check for patterns of data. If you apply the bitwise & operator to the numbers 9 and 14, you get a result of 8. When the binary values of 9 (1001) and 14 (1110) are operated on with a bitwise &, the resulting bit pattern is 8 (1000).

```
1 0 0 1   (9)
& & & &
1 1 1 0   (14)
_____
1 0 0 0   (8)
```

In a C program, you could code this bitwise operation in the following way:

```
result = 9 & 14;
```

The result variable will hold 8, which is the result of the bitwise &. The 9 or 14 (or both) could also be stored in variables, with the same result.

In bitwise truth tables, you can replace the 1 and 0 with True and False, respectively, to understand the result better. For the & (AND) bitwise truth table, both bits being operated on with & must be True for the result to be True. In other words, "True AND True is equal to True."

The Bitwise ¦ (OR)

The ¦ is known as the bitwise OR, or bitwise inclusive OR operator. It sets the resulting bit to 1 if either of the corresponding bits in the operand is 1. It sets the resulting bit to 0 if both of the corresponding bits in the operand are 0. You use the bitwise ¦ (OR) to test whether either bit is set to 1. Table 12.3 shows the truth table that C uses to evaluate the ¦ (OR) operator.

Table 12.3 The Bitwise ¦ (OR) Truth Table

First Bit	OR	Second Bit	Result
1	¦	1	1
1	¦	0	1

Table 12.3	**Continued**		
First Bit	**OR**	**Second Bit**	**Result**
0	¦	1	1
0	¦	0	0

The Bitwise ¦ (OR)

The bitwise ¦ (OR) combines two variables in a bit-by-bit fashion. The syntax is

> *var1 = var2 ¦ var3;*

The result is a variable that has the bitwise "ORed" combination.

When applying the bitwise ¦ operator to the numbers 9 and 14, you get 15. When the binary values of 9 (1001) and 14 (1110) are operated on with a bitwise ¦, the resulting bit pattern is 15 (1111). The reason is that the result's bits are 1 (True) in every position in which a bit is 1 in either of the two numbers.

```
1 0 0 1   (9)
¦ ¦ ¦ ¦
1 1 1 0   (14)
_____
1 1 1 1   (15)
```

In a C program, you could code this bitwise operation like this:

```
result = 9 ¦ 14;
```

The result variable will hold 15, which is the result of the bitwise ¦. The 9 or 14, or both, could also be stored in variables, with the same result.

The ¦ bitwise operator is sometimes called the *inclusive bitwise OR operator*. Either side of the ¦ operator, or both sides, must be 1 (True) for the result to be 1 (True).

The Bitwise ^ (Exclusive OR)

The ^ is known as the bitwise XOR, or bitwise exclusive OR operator. It sets the resulting bit to 1 if either of the corresponding bits in the operand is 1. It sets the resulting bit to 0, however, if both of the corresponding bits in the operand are 1. This distinguishes the ^ operator from the ¦ operator. Like the regular OR, it sets the resulting bit to 0 if both of the corresponding bits in the operand are 0. You use the bitwise ^ (exclusive OR) to test whether either bit is set to 1, but not both. Table 12.4 shows the truth table that C uses to evaluate the ^ (exclusive OR) operator.

Table 12.4	The Bitwise ^ (Exclusive OR) Operator		
First Bit	**XOR**	**Second Bit**	**Result**
1	^	1	0
1	^	0	1
0	^	1	1
0	^	0	0

The Bitwise ^ (exclusive OR)

The bitwise ^ (exclusive OR) combines two variables in a bit-by-bit fashion. The syntax is

```
var1 = var2 ^ var3;
```

The result is a variable that has the bitwise "exclusive ORed" combination.

The bitwise ^, when applied to 9 and 14, produces a 7. The bitwise ^ sets the resulting bit to 1 if one number's bit is on, but not if both are on.

```
1 0 0 1   (9)
^ ^ ^ ^
1 1 1 0   (14)
_____
0 1 1 1   (7)
```

In a C program, you could code this bitwise operation like this:

```
result = 9 ^ 14;
```

The `result` variable has a value of 7, which is the result of the bitwise ^. The 9, the 14, or both could also be stored in variables, with the same result.

The ^ bitwise operator is called the *exclusive bitwise OR* operator. Either side of the ^ operator must be 1 (True) for the result to be 1 (True), but both sides cannot be 1 (True) at the same time.

The Bitwise ~ (1's Complement)

The ~ operator is known as the 1's compliment operator. Unlike the other operators in this section, it operates on only one operand. It reverses each bit in the result to the opposite value of what it was in the operand.

Table 12.5 The Bitwise ~ (1's Complement) Operator		
1's Complement	**Bit**	**Result**
~	1	0
~	0	1

The Bitwise ~ (1's Complement)

The ~ bitwise operator, called the *bitwise 1's complement* operator, reverses each bit to its opposite value.

> *var1 = ~var2;*

The bitwise ~ simply reverses each bit. ~ is a unary bitwise operator because you can apply it to only one value at a time. The bitwise ~ applied to 9 will result in different values, depending on whether you are working on a 16- or 32-bit compiler.

```
~ 1 0 0 1   (9)
_____
  0 1 1 0   (6)
```

In a C program, you could code the ~ bitwise operation like this:

```
unsigned char   uc_result = ~9;
signed char     sc_result = ~9;
unsigned int    ui_result = ~9;
signed int      si_result = ~9;
unsigned long   ul_result = ~9;
signed long     sl_result = ~9;
```

The uc_result variable holds 246, the result of the bitwise ~ on the unsigned char 9. The sc_result variable holds –10, the result of the bitwise ~ on the signed char 9. The ui_result variable holds 65526, the result of the bitwise ~ on the unsigned int 9. The si_result variable holds –10, the result of the bitwise ~ on the signed int 9.

The ul_result variable holds 4294967286, the result of the bitwise ~ on the unsigned long 9.

The sl_result variable holds –10, the result of the bitwise ~ on the signed long 9.

In any case, the 9 could have been stored in a variable, with the same result.

> **Note**
>
> The bitwise 1's complement does *not* make a number negative. The computer uses a different approach to reverse numbers. The bitwise 1's complement simply reverses the bit pattern of numbers.

Using Bitwise Operators for Efficiency

One of the reasons for using the bitwise operators is to improve the efficiency of certain programming activities. You can take advantage of the bitwise operators to perform tests on data that you couldn't perform as efficiently in other ways.

Suppose, for example, that you want to know whether the user typed an odd or even number (assuming that the input is an integer). One way to do this is to use the modulus operator (%) to see whether the remainder, after dividing the input value by 2, is 0 or 1. If the remainder is 0, the number is even. If the remainder is 1, the number is odd. This approach works, of course, but it requires a number of steps to complete the task. If the system that you are writing has a strict performance requirement, you would need to improve on this scheme.

The bitwise operators are more efficient than other operators because bitwise operators directly compare bit patterns without using any mathematical operations. Because a number is even if its bit pattern ends in 0 and odd if its bit pattern ends in 1, you can also test for odd or even numbers by applying the bitwise & to the data and to a binary 1. This technique is more efficient than using the modulus operator. Listing 12.1 tells the user whether the input value is odd or even.

Listing 12.1   The Bitwise &

```
/* Uses a bitwise & to see whether a number is odd or even */

#include <stdio.h>

main()
     {
     int  input;    /* Will hold user's number */

     input = 2;

     if (input & 1) /* True if result is 1; otherwise, it is */
                    /* False (0) */
```

(continues)

Listing 12.1   Continued

```
                    {
                    printf("the number is odd");
                    }
            else
                    {
                    printf( "The number is even\n");
                    }
        return 0;
        }
```

Let's examine how this program works. You begin with the number 2. The bit representation of 2 in a 16-bit integer is `0000000000000010`. This example tests the number by performing a bitwise & (AND) with the integer representation of 1, which is `0000000000000001`.

```
0 0 0 0 0 0 0 0 0 0 0 0 0 0 1 0
& & & & & & & & & & & & & & & &
0 0 0 0 0 0 0 0 0 0 0 0 0 0 0 1
───────────────────────────────
0 0 0 0 0 0 0 0 0 0 0 0 0 0 0 0
```

Here is the output for this program:

```
The number is even
```

The only interesting bit is the least significant bit or the 1's place. Because all of the other bits in the bit representation are 0s, they will automatically make the answer bits 0 in all places except the least significant bit. The 1 in that place will be ANDed to whatever is in that bit position of the top number. If the top number's rightmost bit is 1, the expression will be 1 & 1 = 1. The resulting number will be 0000000000000001, which is the integer 1. If the result is 1, the top number must have been odd.

Using Bitwise Operators for Convenience

Another interesting way to use the bitwise operators is to capitalize a string of characters. The only difference between the bit patterns for uppercase and lowercase characters is bit number 6 (the sixth bit from the right). For lowercase letters, bit 6 is a 1. For uppercase letters, bit 5 is a 0. The following example shows how A and B differ from a and b by a single bit.

ASCII A	01000001	(hex 41, decimal 65)
ASCII a	01100001	(hex 61, decimal 97)

ASCII B	01000010	(hex 42, decimal 66)
ASCII b	01100010	(hex 62, decimal 98)

To convert a character to uppercase, you have to turn off (change to a 0) bit number 6. You can apply a bitwise & to the input character and 223 (which is 11011111 in binary) to turn off bit 6 and convert any input character to its uppercase equivalent.

```
0 1 1 0 0 0 0 1          a
& & & & & & & &
1 1 0 1 1 1 1 1
_____

0 1 0 0 0 0 0 1          A
```

If the number is already in uppercase, this bitwise & will not change it.

```
0 1 0 0 0 0 0 1          A
& & & & & & & &
1 1 0 1 1 1 1 1
_____

0 1 0 0 0 0 0 1          A
```

The 223 (binary 11011111) is called a *bit mask* because it masks off (just as masking tape masks off areas to be painted) bit 6 so that it becomes 0, if it isn't already. Listing 12.2 does this to ensure that the user types uppercase characters when he or she is asked to input initials.

Listing 12.2   A Program that Demonstrates the Use of Bitmasks

```c
/* Converts the input characters to uppercase if they aren't */
/* already */

#include <stdio.h>

#define   BITMASK   (0xDF)        /* 11011111 in binary */

main()
    {
        char    first, middle, last;  /* Will hold user's initials */

        first = 's';
        middle = 'B';
        last = 'p';
```

(continues)

Listing 12.2 Continued

```
/* Ensure that initials are in uppercase
first = first & BITMASK;      /* Turn off bit 6 if */
middle = middle & BITMASK;    /* it isn't already */
last = last & BITMASK;        /* turned off */

printf ( "Your initials are: %c,%c,%c\n",first,middle,last);
return 0;
}
```

You will recall that the #define will do a substitution in place of BITMASK. The problem then becomes

```
0 1 1 1 0 0 1 1          s
& & & & & & & &
1 1 0 1 1 1 1 1
_____
0 1 0 1 0 0 1 1          S


0 1 0 0 0 0 1 0          B
& & & & & & & &
1 1 0 1 1 1 1 1
_____
0 1 0 0 0 0 1 0          B


0 1 1 1 0 0 0 0          p
& & & & & & & &
1 1 0 1 1 1 1 1
_____
0 1 0 1 0 0 0 0          P
```

The following output shows what happens when two of the initials are lowercase letters. The program converts them to uppercase before printing them again. Although there are other ways to convert letters to uppercase, none are as efficient as using the & bitwise operator.

```
Your initials are: S,B,P
```

Compound Bitwise Operators

As with most of the mathematical operators, you can combine the bitwise operators with the equal sign (=) to form *compound bitwise operators*. When you use a bitwise operator, you can shorten the expression by using the compound bitwise operators, shown in table 12.6.

Table 12.6	The Compound Bitwise Operators
Operator	**Description**
&=	Compound bitwise AND assignment
¦=	Compound bitwise inclusive-OR assignment
^=	Compound bitwise exclusive-OR assignment

The preceding example for converting lowercase initials to their uppercase equivalents can be rewritten with compound bitwise & operators, as demonstrated in listing 12.3.

Listing 12.3   A Program that Uses the Uppercase Bitmasks

```
/* Converts the input characters to uppercase if they aren't */
/* already */

#include <stdio.h>

#define   BITMASK    (0xDF)      /* 11011111 in binary */

main()
     {
     char    first, middle, last;  /* Will hold user's initials */


     first = 's';
     middle = 'B';
     last = 'p';

     /* Ensure that initials are in uppercase */
     first &= BITMASK;      /* Turn off bit 6 if it isn't */
     middle &= BITMASK;     /* already turned off */
     last &= BITMASK;

     printf ( "Your initials are: %c,%c,%c\n",first,middle,last);
     return 0;
     }
```

Mathematics of the Binary Bitwise Operators

There are three important mathematical properties of the binary bitwise operators. The first property is associativity, which means that the action of any of the binary bitwise operators on any three objects does not depend on how the three objects are grouped. Note the following examples:

```
(A ¦ B) ¦ C = A ¦ (B ¦ C)
(A & B) & C = A & (B & C)
(A ^ B) ^ C = A ^ (B ^ C)
```

The second property is commutativity, which means that the action of any of the binary bitwise operators on any two objects does not depend on the order in which the objects are given. Note these examples:

```
A ¦ B = B ¦ A
A & B = B & A
A ^ B = B ^ A
```

The third property is that of having an identity value: each of the binary bitwise operators has an identity, which is a value e for which A oper e = e oper A = A, where oper represents the operator. Note some examples:

```
A ¦ 0 = 0 ¦ A = A
A & 1 = 1 & A = A
A ^ 0 = 0 ^ A = A
```

The important thing to remember about this last property is that it applies, as the binary bitwise operators do, bit by bit. Although this isn't a problem for the inclusive- and exclusive-OR operators, it can be a problem for the AND operator. When applying the AND operator, don't forget to include enough 1 bits to fill up the variable. If you don't, you may change bits that you intended to leave alone.

Bitwise Shift Operators

The bitwise shift operators are shown in table 12.7. They shift bits inside a number to the left or right. The number of bits shifted depends on the value to the right of the bitwise shift operator. The formats of the bitwise shift operators are in table 12.7.

Table 12.7 The Bitwise Shift Operators

Operator	Description
<<	Bitwise left shift
>>	Bitwise right shift

The Bitwise << (Shift)

The << operator, called the *bitwise shift* operator, shifts each bit over a certain number of places.

```
value << number_of_bits
value >> number_of_bits
```

The *value* can be an integer or character variable, or a constant. The *number_of_bits* variable determines how many bits will be shifted. The following example shows what happens when the number 157 (binary 10011101) is left-shifted three bits with a bitwise left shift (<<). Notice that each bit "shifts over" to the left three times, and 0s fill in from the right. If this were a bitwise right shift (>>), the 0s would fill in from the left as the rest of the bits are shifted to the right three times.

```
    vvvvv
10011101   (157 decimal)    157 << 3
vvvvv
11101000 (232 decimal)
```

Notice that the shifting of bits will cause information to be lost. The value of the leftmost three bits of the previous example are now gone to the "bit trash can." This is important because if you later shift the bits back to the right, the >> operator zero-fills from the left. Thus

```
    vvvvv
11101000 (232 decimal)
      vvvvv
00011101   (29 decimal)
```

did not return the value to its earlier value.

Caution

The results of bitwise shift operators are not consistent when applied to signed values. On the PC, the sign bit *propagates* with each shift. That is, for every shift position, the sign bit shifts, but the original sign is retained as well. The end result is that negative numbers fill in from the left with 1s and not with 0s when a bitwise right shift is applied to them.

The following program takes two values and shifts them three bits to the left and then to the right. Listing 12.4 illustrates how to code the bitwise left- and right-shift operators.

Listing 12.4   A Program that Demonstrates Bitwise Shift Operators

```
/* Demonstrates bitwise left- and right-shift operators */

#include <stdio.h>

main()
    {
    int    num1 = 25;        /* 00011001 binary */
    int    num2 = 102;       /* 01100110 binary */
    int    shift1, shift2;   /* Will hold shifted numbers */

    shift1 = num1 << 3;      /* Bitwise left shift */
    printf("25 shifted left 3 times is %d\n ", shift1);

    shift2 = num2 << 3;      /* Bitwise left shift */
    printf("102 shifted left 3 times is %d\n ", shift2);

    shift1 = num1 >> 3;      /* Bitwise right shift */
    printf("25 shifted right 3 times is %d\n ", shift1);

    shift2 = num2 >> 3;      /* Bitwise right shift */
    printf("102 shifted right 3 times is %d\n ", shift2);

    return 0;
    }
```

Here is the output for this program:

```
25 shifted left 3 times is 200

102 shifted left 3 times is 816

25 shifted right 3 times is 3

102 shifted right 3 times is 12
```

You should know another useful feature of bitwise shifting. If you bitwise left-shift a variable by a certain number of bit positions, the result is the same as multiplying that same number by a power of 2. In other words, 15 left-shifted 4 times results in the same value as 15 times 2^4, or 15 times 16, which equals 240.

If you bitwise right-shift a number by a certain number of bit positions, the result is the same as dividing that same number by a power of 2. In other words, 64 right-shifted by 2 results in the same value as 64 divided by 2^2, or 64 divided by 4, which equals 16.

If you have to multiply or divide a variable by a power of 2, you can do it much faster by simply shifting the number. In fact, this is an optimization that the C compiler frequently uses internally. Listing 12.5 illustrates this.

Listing 12.5   Performing Math by Shifting

```
/* Demonstrates multiplication and division by */
/* bitwise shifting */

#include <stdio.h>

main()
        {
 int    num1 = 16;        /* Numbers to be shifted */
 int    num3 = 16;
 int    num4 = 0x8000;

        num1 = num1 << 4;     /* Multiply num1 by 16 */
        num3 = num3 >> 2;     /* Divide num3 by 4 */
        num4 = num4 >> 1;     /* divide num4 by 2 */

        printf("16 multiplied by 16 is %d\n",num1);
        printf("16 divided by 4 is %d\n", num3);
        printf("0x8000 divided by 2 is 0x %x\n",num4);


        return 0;
        }
```

The output from listing 12.5 looks like the following:

```
16 multiplied by 16 is 256
16 divided by 4 is 4
0x8000 divided by 2 is 0x 4000
```

Look at this example in more detail. The first shift operation was

```
num1 = num1 << 4;     /* Multiply num1 by 16 */
```

num1 was initialized to 16, whose bits look like the following:

```
0000 0000 0001 0000  (16 decimal)
```

If you shift it four times, it becomes

```
0000 0001 0000 0000  (256 decimal)
```

The second example is similar:

```
num3 = num3 >> 2;     /* Multiply num3 by 4 */
```

num3 was initialized to 16, whose bits look like the following:

```
0000 0000 0001 0000  (16 decimal)
```

If you shift it left two times, it becomes:

`0000 0000 0001 0100` (4 decimal)

The third example does the same thing, but with hexadecimal numbers:

```
num4 = num4 >> 1;      /* divide num4 by 2 */
```

num4 was initialized to 0x 8000, whose bits look like the following:

`1000 0000 0000 0000` (0x 8000) (32768 decimal)

If you shift it left one time, it becomes

`0100 0000 0000 0000` (0x 4000) (16384 decimal)

This last example is one demonstration of how convenient hexadecimal format is in dealing with bits. Instead of numbers like 32768, you can use 0x 8000.

Compound Bitwise Shift Operators

As with most of the mathematical operators, you can combine the bitwise operators with the equal sign (=) to form *compound bitwise shift operators*. When you want to update the value of a variable by using a bitwise shift operator, you can shorten the expression by using the compound bitwise operators, shown in table 12.8.

Table 12.8 The Compound Bitwise Shift Operators	
Operator	**Description**
<<=	Compound bitwise left shift
>>=	Compound bitwise right shift

Listing 12.6 demonstrates how the previous example could be shortened a little by using the compound operators.

Listing 12.6 Compound Bitwise Shift Operators

```
/* Demonstrates multiplication and division by */
/* bitwise shifting */

#include <stdio.h>

main()
    {
```

```
int    num1 = 16;        /* Numbers to be shifted */
int    num3 = 16;
int    num4 = 0x8000;

       num1 <<= 4;       /* Multiply num1 by 16 */
       num3 >>= 2;       /* Divide num3 by 4 */
       num4 >>= 1;       /* divide num4 by 2 */

       printf("16 multiplied by 16 is %d\n",num1);
       printf("16 divided by 4 is %d\n", num3);
       printf("0x8000 divided by 2 is 0x %x\n",num4);


       return 0;
       }
```

The output from this example looks like this:

```
16 multiplied by 16 is 256
16 divided by 4 is 4
0x8000 divided by 2 is 0x c000
```

You will notice that this output is exactly the same as the output of the preceding example.

The Compound Bitwise << = (Shift)
The << = operator, called the *bitwise shift* operator, shifts each bit over a certain number of places.

```
       num1 <<= 4;       /* Multiply num1 by 16 */
       num2 >>= 2;       /* Divide num2 by 4 */
       num3 >>= 1;       /* divide num3 by 2 */
```

The compound bitwise shift operator is used in a manner similar to the other compound operators in C.

Summary

Because the bitwise operators work at the bit level, they are not often used in application programs. You must be comfortable with the binary numbering system before you can fully understand the operations of the bitwise operators. However, the bitwise operators offer a very efficient method of changing individual bits or groups of bits in variables. With these operators, you can test for odd and even numbers, multiply and divide by powers of two, and perform other tasks for which you would normally use less efficient operators and commands.

The bitwise operators, despite their efficiency, do not always lend themselves to readable code. Generally, most people reserve them for systems-level programming and use the easier-to-read, higher-level operators for most data processing.

Index

Symbols

! NOT operator, 43-44
!= (not equal) operator, 40
& (ampersand)
   address operator, 153
   bitwise AND operator,
   218-219
      listing 12.1, 223-224
&& AND operator, 43-44
&= bitwise compound AND
   operator, 227
(- -) decrement operator,
   41, 88
* (asterisk) as indirection
   operator, 152
++ increment operator, 41
< (less than) operator, 40
<< bitwise left shift operator,
   229
<<= compound bitwise left
   shift operator, 232-233
<= (less than or equal)
   operator, 40
= (equals) operator, 40
== equality operator, 70
> (greater than) operator, 40
>= (greater than or equal)
   operator, 40
>> bitwise right shift operator,
   229
>>= compound bitwise right
   shift operator, 232
^ (caret) bitwise exclusive OR
   operator, 218, 220-221
^= bitwise compound
   exclusive OR operator, 227
{ } (braces) in functions, 18
¦ (pipe) bitwise inclusive OR
   operator, 218-220
¦= bitwise compound
   inclusive OR operator, 227
¦¦ OR operator, 43-44
~ (tilde) bitwise 1's
   complement operator, 218,
   221-223

A

abort( ) function, 116
abs( ) function, 114
accessing
   array elements, 162-165
   structure elements, 176
acos( ) function, 114
addition, 38
AND (&) operator, 218-219
ANSI (American National
   Standards Institute), 6
argc parameter, 130
arguments (functions), 124
   passing by reference, 156
   passing by value, 155
argv parameter, 130
arithmetic operators, 38-39
ARRAY.C (listing 3.5), 37
arrays, 32-37
   bounds checking, 34
   character arrays, pointers,
   159-160
   dimensions, 33

loops, 99-101
multi-dimensional, 35
   initializing, 35-36
   pointers, 169-171
one-dimensional, 33
   initializing, 34-35
   pointers, 162-165
passing to functions,
   125-129
reading, 213-214
referring to elements,
   162-165
string variables, 36
structures, 176-178
two-dimensional, 35
   pointers, 170-171
writing, 213-214
ASCII code, 29
asctime( ) function, 115
asin( ) function, 114
assert( ) function, 117
ASSERT.H, 111, 117
assignment operators, 38
atan( ) function, 114
AVG.C (listing 6.4), 89-90

B

BACK.C (listing 11.8), 206-207
Backspace key, 50
Bell Telephone Laboratories,
   Inc., 5
beta testing, 10
binary bitwise operators, 228
bitmask demonstration
   (listing 12.2), 225-226
bits, 218